International
English

International English

A Guide to Varieties of Standard English

Peter Trudgill and
Jean Hannah

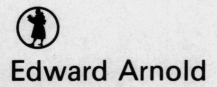

Edward Arnold

Copyright © 1982 Peter Trudgill and Jean Hannah

First published 1982 by
Edward Arnold (Publishers) Ltd
41 Bedford Square, London WC1B 3DQ

British Library Cataloguing in Publication Data
Trudgill, Peter
    International English.
    1. English language—Grammar
    I. Title   II. Hannah, Jean
    428.2   PE1112

ISBN 0-7131-6362-3

**This book is accompanied by a recording, which is available on cassette
only.**

Filmset by Willmer Brothers Limited, Birkenhead, Merseyside
Printed in Great Britain by Richard Clay (The Chaucer Press) Limited,
Bungay, Suffolk

Contents

Acknowledgements   ix
Symbols   x

1 Varieties of Standard English   1
  1.1 The Two Main Standard Varieties   1
  1.2 The Spread of English   4

2 English, Australasian, South African and Welsh English   9
  2.1 The RP Accent   9
  2.2 Australian, New Zealand and South African English   15
  2.3 Welsh English   27

3 The Pronunciation of North American English   31
  3.1 North American English Vowels   31
  3.2 North American English Consonants   35
  3.3 Variation within North American English   36
  3.4 Non-systematic Differences between North
     American English and English English Pro-
     nunciation   40
  3.5 Stress Differences   41
  3.6 Differences between American English and
     Canadian English Pronunciation   42

**4 English and North American English: Grammatical,
Orthographical and Lexical Differences**   43
  4.1 Grammatical Differences   43
  4.2 Spelling and Punctuation Differences   69
  4.3 Vocabulary Differences   73

5 Scottish and Irish English   81
  5.1 Scottish English   81
  5.2 English in Ireland   88

6 Other Varieties of English   95
  6.1 English-based Creoles   95
  6.2 Non-native Varieties of English   99

Glossary   113
Selected References and Further Reading   117
The Recording   121
The Reading Passage   123
Index   125

For Mum, Dad, and Mom

Acknowledgements

Very many people have helped with the writing of this book, by supplying information, reading and correcting earlier versions of the typescript, and by advising on content and format. We cannot list them all, but are grateful to all of them. We would particularly like to thank the following: J. Allwood, L. Bauer, A. Bell, J. Bernard, K. Bhat, C. Biggs, J. K. Chambers, J. Clark, A. Davison, J. A. Edmondson, J. R. Edwards, V. K. Edwards, S. Foldvik, C. W. Kisseberth, Bh. Krishnamurti, L. Lanham, S. Millar, J. Milroy, J. L. Morgan, D. Sutcliffe, A. R. Thomas, J. Ure, S. K. Verma, and J. C. Wells. We are also very grateful to colleagues in the Department of Linguistic Science of Reading University, who helped in many ways.

Symbols

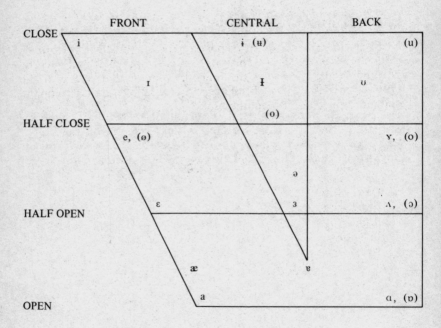

General Symbols

[ ] — phonetic transcription (indicates actual pronunciation)
/ / — phonemic transcription
~ — 'alternates with'
* — indicates ungrammatical sentence
? — indicates sentence of questionable grammaticality

English Vowel Symbols

A vowel can be described by its position on two dimensions: *open* vs. *close*, and *front* vs. *back*. This position corresponds roughly to the position in the mouth of the highest point of the tongue in the production of that vowel. Presence of lip rounding is indicated on the diagram opposite by parentheses.

Diacritics
  ⊤ more open
  ⊢ more back
  ⊥ more close
  ⊣ more front
  : long
  · half-long
  ′ stress

English Consonant Phonemes

/p/	as	*p*	in	*peat*
/t/	as	*t*	in	*treat*
/č/	as	*ch*	in	*cheat*
/k/	as	*k*	in	*kite*
/b/	as	*b*	in	*bite*
/d/	as	*d*	in	*date*
/ǰ/	as	*j*	in	*jute*
/g/	as	*g*	in	*gate*
/f/	as	*f*	in	*fate*
/θ/	as	*th*	in	*thought*
/s/	as	*s*	in	*site*
/š/	as	*sh*	in	*sheet*
/h/	as	*h*	in	*hate*
/v/	as	*v*	in	*vote*
/ð/	as	*th*	in	*that*
/z/	as	*z*	in	*zoo*
/ž/	as	*s*	in	*vision*
/l/	as	*l*	in	*late*
/r/	as	*r*	in	*rate*
/w/	as	*w*	in	*wait*
/j/	as	*y*	in	*yet*
/m/	as	*m*	in	*meet*
/n/	as	*n*	in	*neat*
/ŋ/	as	*ng*	in	*long*

Other Consonant Symbols

[ʔ]	glottal stop
[ɫ]	velarized or 'dark' *l*, as in RP *all*
[ɬ]	voiceless lateral fricative
[ɹ]	post-alveolar frictionless continuant, as *r* in RP *right*
[ɾ]	alveolar flap, *r* in Spanish *pero*
[ç]	voiceless palatal fricative
[x]	voiceless velar fricative, as *ch* in German *Nacht*
[ɸ]	voiceless bilabial fricative
[ʍ]	voiceless *w*
[ɖ]	voiced alveolar flap
Ç̱	dental consonant
Ç̣	retroflex consonant
Cʰ	aspirated consonant
Ç̦	syllabic consonant

1

Varieties of Standard English

The subject of this book is *Standard English*, the variety of the English language which is normally employed in writing and normally spoken by 'educated' speakers of the language. It is also, of course, the variety of English that students of English as a Foreign or Second Language (EFL/ESL) are taught when receiving formal instruction. The term *Standard English* often refers to grammar and vocabulary (*dialect*) but not to pronunciation (*accent*). Thus:

> *I haven't got any*

is a sentence of Standard English, no matter how it is pronounced, while

> *I ain't got none*

is not a sentence of Standard English, consisting as it does of forms used in many non-standard dialects. In this book, however, we shall also be dealing with those accents of English that are normally used by speakers of Standard English and are therefore most closely associated with this variety. Note, too, that Standard English includes informal as well as formal styles:

> *I haven't got a bloody clue* is Standard English, while
> *I ain't got no idea* is not.

1.1 The Two Main Standard Varieties

Traditionally, schools and universities in Europe—and in many other parts of the world—have taught that variety of English often referred to as 'British English'. As far as grammar and vocabulary are concerned, this generally means Standard English as it is normally written and spoken by educated speakers in England and, with minor differences, in Wales, Scotland, Northern Ireland, The Republic of Ireland, Australia, New Zealand and South Africa. As far as pronunciation is concerned, it means something much more restrictive, for the RP ('Received Pronunciation') accent which is taught to foreigners is actually used by perhaps only 3 per cent to 5 per cent of the population of England. The RP accent has its origins in the south-east of England but is currently a social accent associated with the BBC, the Public Schools in England, and with members of the upper-middle and upper classes. It is considered a prestigious accent in the whole of the British Isles and British Commonwealth, but it is for the most part an accent associated only with England. For this reason, in this book we shall refer to the combination of British Standard English grammar and vocabulary with the RP accent as *English* English (EngEng) rather than British English.

The other form of Standard English that is widely taught to students of EFL and ESL we shall refer to as North American English (NAmEng), meaning English as it is written and spoken by educated speakers in the United States of America and Canada. (If we wish to distinguish between these two North American varieties, we will write United States English (USEng) and Canadian English (CanEng).) NAmEng is, naturally, taught to students learning English in North America, and also to those in many parts of Latin America and other areas of the world.

Until recently, many European universities and colleges not only taught EngEng but actually *required* it from their students; i.e. other varieties of Standard English were not allowed. This was the result of a conscious decision, often, that some norm needed to be established and that confusion would arise if teachers offered conflicting models. Lately, many universities have come to relax this requirement, recognizing that their students are as likely (if not more likely) to encounter NAmEng as EngEng, especially since some European students study for a time in North America. Many universities therefore now permit students to speak and write *either* EngEng *or* NAmEng, *so long as they are consistent* (or that, at least, is the theory).

We feel that this is a step in the right direction but it is also somewhat unrealistic. For example, it is not reasonable to expect a Dutch student of English who has learnt EngEng at school and then studied for a year in the USA to return to the Netherlands with anything other than some mixture of NAmEng and EngEng. This is exactly what happens to British or American native speakers who cross the Atlantic for any length of time. Given that the ideal which foreign students are aiming at is native-like competence in English, we feel there is nothing reprehensible about such a mixture and that tolerating it is by no means necessarily a bad thing. Neither is it necessarily bad or confusing for schoolchildren to be exposed to more than one model.

In any case, whatever the exact form of the requirements placed on students of English by different universities and in different countries, it is clear that exposure to and/or recognition of the legitimacy of these two varieties of Standard English in English language-learning is likely to bring with it certain problems. Both those teachers wishing to insist on a rigid use of only, say, EngEng to the exclusion of NAmEng, and those wishing to permit use of both varieties, need to be quite clear about which forms occur in which variety. For example, teachers of EngEng (whether they are native speakers or not) who encounter expressions such as 'First of all . . ., second of all . . .' or 'I did it in five minutes time' in a student's work are likely to regard these as typical learner's mistakes unless they are aware that these forms are perfectly normal in some varieties of NAmEng. Similarly, teachers of NAmEng may mark as incorrect certain forms which are perfectly acceptable in EngEng, such as 'I might do' and 'I'll give it him'.

Students in many parts of Asia and Africa are more likely to come into contact with Australian English (AusEng), New Zealand English (NZEng—jointly AusNZEng), or South African English (SAfEng) than with EngEng or NAmEng. It is useful for students and teachers of English in these areas, too, to be aware of the differences between their standard variety of English and the other standard varieties.

It is our hope that this book and recording will provide at least a partial solution to the problem of recognizing and coping with differences among the standard varieties of English by covering differences at the levels of phonetics, phonology, grammar and vocabulary. (Differences in intonation patterns, fine phonetic detail, and regional and non-standard varieties are referred to in the Further Reading section; little is known about differences in discourse features, but some remarks are included.) This information should be of assistance in particular to teachers and students of EFL. Teachers need to be aware of differences in order to present one or more standard variety clearly and to assess students' work, while non-native speakers who have learnt or are learning one variety of English should find it useful to increase their ability to understand other varieties of spoken and written Standard English. This book can also be of help to native speakers of English, for even though native speakers understand many more varieties of their language than they speak, differences in accent and subtle or unexpected differences in dialect can hamper understanding for them, too. Finally, this material should also be of interest to anyone working in English linguistics or dialectology.

1.2   The Spread of English

The English language was originally spoken in England and south-eastern Scotland, and by the middle-ages it was also spoken in most other areas of southern and eastern Scotland. The language was introduced into Ireland from England—mainly into southern Ireland from the west of England—in mediæval times, but was not widely spoken there until the eighteenth or nineteenth century; and it was brought to North America in the seventeenth and eighteenth centuries. (It is therefore not surprising that there are still many resemblences in pronunciation between current NAmEng, Irish English (IrEng), and the English spoken in the West of England.) Also during the seventeenth century, English was imported into northern areas of Ireland from Scotland. (The English of Northern Ireland (NIrEng) therefore has similarities both with Scottish English (ScotEng) and Scots (Scottish dialect—see chapter 5), and with the English spoken in the Republic of Ireland (SIrEng).)

English was not exported to South Africa, Australia and New Zealand to any extent until later—the eighteenth and nineteenth centuries—and the main linguistic influences in these cases seem to be from south-eastern England. SAfEng, AusEng and NZEng are therefore phonologically similar to RP and to one another.

English also became widespread in Wales at about the same time. Welsh English (WEng) is therefore also structurally very similar to EngEng, although the influence of Welsh has played a role in its formation and has led to the development of a variety that is phonetically probably not so similar to EngEng as are AusNZEng and SAfEng.

We have attempted to portray the relationships among the pronunciation of all these varieties in figure 1.1. This diagram is somewhat arbitrary and slightly misleading (there are, for example, accents of USEng which are closer to RP than to mid-western US English), but it does show the two main types of pronunciation: an 'English' type (EngEng, WEng, SAfEng, AusEng, NZEng) and an 'American' type (USEng, CanEng), with IrEng falling somewhere between the two and ScotEng being somewhat by itself.

Lexically and grammatically the split between the 'English' and 'American' types is somewhat neater, with USEng and CanEng being opposed on most counts to the rest of the English-speaking world. This generalization holds true in spite of the fact that each variety has its individual lexical and grammatical characteristics and that, for instance, at some points where ScotEng and IrEng grammar differ from EngEng, they closely resemble NAmEng.

The 'English' types of English, which do not differ greatly from EngEng, will be treated first in this book and are discussed in

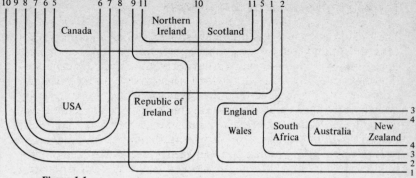

Figure 1.1

KEY

1. /ɑː/ rather than /æ/ in *path* etc.
2. absence of non-prevocalic /r/
3. close vowels for /æ/and/ɛ/, monophthongization of /ai/and/ɑu/
4. front [aː] for /ɑː/ in *part* etc.
5. absence of contrast of /ɒ/ and /ɔː/ as in *cot* and *caught*
6. /æ/ rather than /ɑː/ in *can't* etc.
7. absence of contrast of /ɒ/ and /ɑː/ as in *bother* and *father*
8. consistent voicing of intervocalic /t/
9. unrounded [ɑ] in *pot*
10. syllabic /r/ in *bird*
11. absence of contrast of /ʊ/ and /uː/ as in *pull* and *pool*

chapter 2. The 'American' types, and the relatively larger amount of differences between them and the 'English' types, are dealt with, necessarily at greater length, in chapters 3 and 4. ScotEng and IrEng, which we classify as neither 'English' nor 'American' types, are discussed in chapter 5.

Of native varieties of English spoken in other areas, Bermudian English appears to be more of the 'American' type, while the English spoken on Tristan da Cunha and the Falkland Islands appears to be more of the 'English' type, the latter bearing some resemblances to AusEng.

English-based pidgins and creoles have a much more complex history than other English varieties. They include the Atlantic pidgins, creoles and creolized varieties of the Caribbean area, the Atlantic coasts of North, Central and Latin America, the island of St. Helena, and West Africa; and the Pacific varieties of Papua-New Guinea, the Solomon Islands, and the New Hebrides, among others. (American Black Vernacular English also has a creole history, and there are transplanted off-shoots of it in Liberia and the Dominican

Native English-Speaking Areas

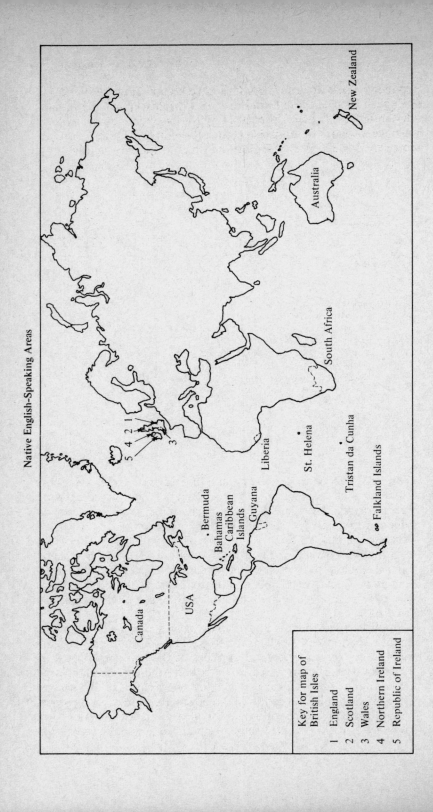

New Zealand

Australia

South Africa

Liberia

St. Helena

Tristan da Cunha

Falkland Islands

Bermuda

Bahamas

Caribbean
Islands

Guyana

Canada

USA

1 England
2 Scotland
3 Wales
4 Northern Ireland
5 Republic of Ireland

Key for map of
British Isles

Republic.) There are also well-established second-language varieties of English such as those found in Africa, Malaysia and the Indian sub-continent. Chapter 6 discusses English-based creoles and second language varieties of English in general, with specific reference to Jamaican English, West African English, and Indian English.

2
English, Australasian, South African and Welsh English

In this chapter we discuss the 'English' types of English and point out the relationships and differences between them. At certain points we also contrast and compare the 'English' types with NAmEng, but this is done in more detail in chapters 3 and 4.

2.1 The RP Accent

As we have already mentioned, the accent which is normally taught to students who are studying EngEng is the accent known as RP. (This is the accent which is described, for example, in Gimson (1980) and in most other English textbooks.) There are a number of advantages to learning this particular accent. First, while it originated in the south-east of England, it is now a genuinely regionless accent within Britain; i.e. if speakers have an RP accent, you cannot tell which area of Britain they come from (which is not the case for any other type of British accent). This means that this accent is likely to be encountered and understood throughout the country. Second, RP is the accent which is used most often in radio and television broadcasts in England, so a student will have many opportunities to listen to it.

There are also disadvantages to learning only RP. First, it is an accent used natively by only 3 per cent to 5 per cent of the population of England. This means that students arriving in England for the first time may have difficulty—sometimes a great deal of difficulty—understanding the other 95 per cent to 97 per cent of the population. (One book which attempts to help with this problem is Hughes and Trudgill (1979).) Second, while RP is not a regional accent, it *is* a social accent, associated particularly with the upper-middle and upper classes (and those who aspire to those classes). Foreigners who are very successful at acquiring an RP accent may therefore be reacted to as if they were upper-class (and the reaction might not *always* be favourable!). Thirdly, the RP accent is probably rather more difficult for many foreigners to acquire than, say, a Scottish accent, since RP has a large number of diphthongs and a not particularly close relationship to English orthography.

2.1.1   The RP Vowel System

The RP vowel system is presented below in table 2.1 and can also be heard on the recording. While RP does not have any regional variation, as we have said, it does have variation of another type. In particular, there is variation between what some writers have called 'conservative' and 'advanced' RP (see Gimson (1980) and Wells (1982)). For the most part this reflects linguistic changes that are currently taking place in RP, with 'conservative' pronunciations being most typical of older speakers and 'advanced' pronunciations

Table 2.1   The RP Vowel System*

/ɪ/	bid, very, mirror, wanted, horses, honest
/ɛ/	bed, merry
/æ/	bad, marry
/ɒ/	pot, long, cough, horrid
/ʌ/	putt, hurry
/ʊ/	put
/iː/	bee
/ei/	bay
/ai/	buy
/ɔi/	boy
/uː/	boot
/ou/	boat
/au/	bout
/ɪə/	peer, idea
/ɛə/	pair, Mary
/ʊə/	poor
/ɔə/	pore
/ɔː/	paw, port, talk, boring
/ɑː/	bard, path, dance, half, banana, father, calm
/ɜː/	bird, furry
/ə/	about, sofa, butter
/aiə/	fire
/auə/	tower

* *The words in table 2.1 are also used in the recording for WIEng, WAfEng and IndEng (see page 121).*

typical of younger speakers. Some of these differences are the following:

1   As in a number of other accents, the distinction between /ɔə/ and /ɔː/ is now lost for very many speakers, with /ɔə/ becoming monophthongized. A more recent, but by now also wide-spread development, is the loss of /ʊə/ and the merger of this diphthong, also, with /ɔː/. (This latter change for some speakers has affected

some words but not others, so that *sure* may be /šɔ:/ but *poor*, /puə/.)
The current situation with respect to these vowels is something like
this:

	paw	*pore*	*poor*
Older speakers	/ɔ:/	/ɔə/	/uə/
Middle-aged speakers	/ɔ:/	/ɔ:/	/uə/
Younger speakers	/ɔ:/	/ɔ:/	/ɔ:/

2   There is a strong tendency, perhaps part of the same process
whereby /ɔə/ > /ɔ:/, for original triphthongs formed from /ai/ and
/au/ plus /ə/ to be pronounced as monophthongs; e.g. *tower*
/tauə/ > /tɑ:/. This process can be labelled *smoothing* (see Wells
(1982)).

3   Where orthographic *o* occurs before the voiceless fricatives /f/,
/θ/, /s/, older speakers sometimes pronounce the vowel as /ɔ:/, e.g. *off*
/ɔ:f/, *froth* /frɔ:θ/, *lost* /lɔ:st/. This pronunciation is currently dying
out in RP and being replaced by /ɒ/. Words like *salt* and *fault* may
also be pronounced with /ɔ:/, but are often pronounced with /ɒ/, too,
by younger speakers.

4   Conservative RP has a back vowel [u:] in words like *boot*, but
for younger speakers the vowel may increasingly be fronted in the
direction of [ʉ:] except, often, before /l/, as in *fool*.

5   The diphthong /ou/ of *boat* varies considerably, ranging from [ɔʊ]
among conservative speakers to [øʉ] among some advanced
speakers. Perhaps the most neutral pronunciation is around [əʊ].

6   The diphthong /ɛə/ of *pair* is very often monophthongized to [ɛ:]
(cf. 1 and 2 above).

7   Words like *suit* may be pronounced either /su:t/ or /sju:t/. The
tendency is for middle-aged and younger speakers to omit the /j/ after
/s/ before /u:/, but this tendency is much stronger in some words, e.g.
super, *Susan*, than in others, e.g. *suit*. Word-internally, /j/ tends to be
retained, as in *assume* /əsju:m/. There is also fluctuation after /l/:
word-initially *lute* /lu:t/ is normal, but it is possible to pronounce, e.g.
illusion as /ɪlju:žn/.

2.1.2   Vowels in Near-RP Accents

Since RP speakers make up a very small percentage of the English
population, many native speakers working as teachers of English are
not native speakers *of RP*. If they are from the south of England,
particularly the south-east, it is likely that their accents will closely
resemble RP (especially if they are of middle-class origin), but not be
identical to it. Typical differences between the RP vowel system and
many near-RP south-of-England accents are the following:

1   The /i:/ of *bee*, rather than the /ɪ/ of *bid*, occurs in the final syllable

of *very*, *many*, etc. in the near-RP accents. (In this respect, these accents resemble NAmEng, SAfEng and AusNZEng).

2   The fronting of /u:/ towards [ʉ:] is more widespread than in RP. Thus the allophone of /u:/ before /l/, which is not fronted in either type of accent, is, in near-RP, markedly different from those allophones that occur in all other environments. Unlike advanced RP, this variation of allophones with respect to /l/ also occurs with the diphthong /ou/. Thus:

	rude	rule	code	coal
Conservative RP	[ruːd]	[ruːɫ]	[kɔud]	[kɔuɫ]
Advanced RP	[rʉːd]	[ruːɫ]	[køʉd]	[køʉɫ]
Near-RP, southern	[rʉːd]	[ruːɫ]	[køud]	[kɔuɫ]

3   The vowel /ɪ/ in unstressed syllables in RP often corresponds to /ə/ in near-RP accents. The actual distribution of /ɪ/ and /ə/ varies considerably among the different near-RP accents. By way of illustration, there are some near-RP accents which have /ɪ/ *in honest*, *village*, but /ə/ in *wanted*, *horses*. In these accents, therefore, the RP distinction between *roses* /rouzɪz/ and *Rosa's* /rouzəz/ (also found in many NAmEng accents) does not occur, both forms being /rouzəz/.

4   Speakers with northern near-RP accents are likely to differ from RP in one important phonological respect. Like RP, they have a contrast between /æ/ and /ɑ:/ as demonstrated by the following pairs:

/æ/	/ɑ:/
pat	*part*
Pam	*palm*
match	*march*

However, there are two groups of words where RP has /ɑ:/ but northern accents have /æ/. These are:
(a) words in which RP has /ɑ:/ where orthographic *a* is followed by the voiceless fricatives /f/, /θ/, or /s/: *laugh, path, grass*;
(b) words in which RP has /ɑ:/ where orthographic *a* is followed by the nasal clusters /nt/, /ns/, /nš/, /nd/ and /mp/: *plant, dance, branch, demand, sample.* (Note that southern EngEng has *branch* as /brɑ:nš/, northern EngEng /brænč/.)

2.1.3   RP Consonants

1   /l/. One feature of the RP accent, which it shares with many other EngEng accents and those of other 'English' varieties but is not found in NAmEng, ScotEng or IrEng, concerns the positional allophones of the consonant *l*. Syllable-initial /l/ as in *lot* is 'clear', i.e.

pronounced with the body of the tongue raised towards the hard palate, giving a front vowel resonance, while syllable-final /l/ as in *hill* and syllabic /l/ as in *bottle* are 'dark' or velarized, i.e. pronounced with the body of the tongue raised towards the soft palate, giving a back-vowel resonance. Thus *lull* /lʌl/ is pronounced [lʌɫ]. (This difference also holds in AusNZEng. For NAmEng, IrEng and ScotEng, see chapters 3 and 5.) Note that in certain non-RP south-of-England accents, [ɫ] may be considerably darker than in RP or even become vocalized, e.g. *hill* [hɪʊ].

2 /ʍ/. Most EngEng accents have lost the original /w/:/ʍ/ contrast as in *witch* : *which*, *Wales* : *whales*. This is for the most part true also of RP, but there are some (especially older) RP speakers who still preserve it, and one suspects this is often the result of a conscious decision and effort to do so.

3 [ʔ]. In many varieties of English in the British Isles (i.e. EngEng, NIrEng, ScotEng), the consonant /t/ may be realized as a glottal stop [ʔ], except at the beginning of a stressed syllable. Thus:

top	[top]
between	[bɪtwiːn]
bitter	[bɪtə ~ bɪʔə]
fit	[fɪt ~ fɪʔ]

In RP itself the glottal stop can appear only in the following two environments:

(a) as a realization of syllable-final /t/ before a following consonant, as in:

fit them	[fɪtðəm ~ fɪʔðəm]
batman	[bætmn̩ ~ bæʔmn̩]

This is a relatively recent development in RP and is most often heard from younger speakers. It is variable in its occurrence and occurs more frequently before some consonants (e.g. /m/) than others (e.g. /h/). In RP /t/ is *not* realized as [ʔ] between two vowels in environments such as *bitter* or *fit us*.

(b) [ʔ] occurs before /č/ and in certain consonant clusters, as in *church* [čɜːʔč], *box* [bɒʔks], *simply* [sɪmʔplɪ], where it is known as 'glottal reinforcement'.

Neither of these types of pronunciation is normally taught to foreigners, but students should be aware of them. It is probable that the occurrence of [ʔ] in words like those in (b), in particular, helps lead to the impression many North Americans have that the RP accent sounds 'clipped'; and that its absence in either environment contributes to the 'foreignness' of non-native accents.

4 /r/

(a) As is well-known, some English accents are 'rhotic' or 'r-ful' and others are 'non-rhotic' or 'r-less'. Rhotic accents are those which actually pronounce /r/, corresponding to orthographic *r*, in words like *far* and *farm*: /fɑ:r/, /fɑ:rm/. (The consonant *r* in these positions—word-finally before a pause, or before a consonant—is known as 'non-prevocalic /r/'.) Non-rhotic accents do not have /r/ in these positions and have e.g. *farm* as /fɑ:m/. (Nearly all accents, of course, rhotic and non-rhotic, have /r/ pronounced before a vowel, as in *rob*, *sorry*.) RP is a non-rhotic accent, and thus has no contrasts of the type:

> ma   mar
> cawed   cord

(b) Speakers of many non-rhotic accents, while not pronouncing orthographic *r* word-finally before a pause or before a consonant, do pronounce it where there is a following word which begins with a vowel:

> *It's not far*   no /r/
> *He's far behind*   no /r/
> *She's far away*   /r/ pronounced

That is to say, words like *far* have two pronunciations, depending on whether or not there is a following vowel. In non-rhotic accents, the /r/ that occurs in *far away*, etc. is known as *linking* /r/. The RP accent has this linking /r/. Failure by students to pronounce linking /r/ does not usually affect comprehension but may result in their sounding stilted or foreign. (Note, however, that not all non-rhotic accents of English have linking /r/—see table 2.2 below.)

(c) As a further development, and by analogy with linking /r/, there are now many accents of English in which an /r/ is inserted before a following vowel even though there is no *r* in the spelling. This /r/ is known as *intrusive* /r/. In many EngEng accents it occurs in environments such as:

> *draw*   /drɔ:/   *draw up*   /drɔ:rʌp/
>   on the pattern of *soar—soar up*
>
> *pa*   /pɑ:/   *pa and*   /pɑ:rənd/
>   on the pattern of *far—far and*
>
> *China* /čainə/   *China and* /čainərənd/
>   on the pattern of *finer—finer and*
>
> *idea*   /aidɪə/   *idea and* /aidɪərənd/
>   on the pattern of *near—near and*

It can also occur word-internally, as in *drawing* /drɔ:rɪŋ/. Obviously, what has happened historically is that the loss of /r/ before consonants in non-rhotic accents, which led to alternations of the *far—far away* type, has become reinterpreted as a rule which inserts /r/ after the vowels /ɑ:/, /ɔ:/, /ɜ:/, /ɪə/, /ɛə/, and /ə/, before a following vowel.

Does RP have intrusive /r/? Many textbooks suggest that it does not. The actual situation, however, is that today most RP speakers, particularly younger ones, do have intrusive /r/ after /ə/, as in *China and*, and after /ɪə/, as in *idea of*. In these environments, pronunciations without /r/ sound stilted or foreign. In other environments, as in *law and, pa and, drawing*, while intrusive /r/ does occur in the non-RP accents, particularly those spoken in the southeast of England, it is still somewhat conspicuous in RP. Intrusive /r/ in these environments is socially stigmatized to a certain extent—the /r/ is felt to be 'incorrect' because it does not correspond to an *r* in the spelling—and many RP speakers try to avoid it, quite frequently without being entirely successful. For example, many BBC newsreaders, when reading a phrase such as *law and order*, have to pause or insert a glottal stop before *and* in order not to pronounce an /r/.

Table 2.2 gives some indication of the occurrence of these different /r/s in different varieties of English:

Table 2.2   */r/*

	for Non-prevocalic /r/	*for it* Linking /r/	*saw it* Intrusive /r/
RP	no	yes	variable
Non-RP, South EngEng	no	yes	yes
ScotEng	yes	—	no
IrEng	yes	—	no
CanEng	yes	—	no
Mid-West USEng	yes	—	no
East New England USEng	no	yes	yes
New York City USEng	variable	yes	variable
South East USEng	no	no	no
AusEng	no	yes	yes
NZEng	no	yes	yes
SAfEng	no	no	no

2.2 Australian, New Zealand and South African English

We now turn to an examination of the other 'English' types of English: those found in Australia, New Zealand and South Africa. Strange as it may seem to those who speak these varieties, many people from other parts of the English-speaking world often have difficulty in telling one from the other—and indeed, as we have - already suggested, there are many similarities between them in spite of the thousands of miles that separate the three countries.

The sociolinguistic situation (as far as English is concerned) is also similar in the three countries. There is, for example, very little regional variation in the English used, especially if compared to the amount of regional variation found in Britain—although there is probably rather more variation of this type in SAfEng than in the other two countries. (For the most part, regional variation in AusNZEng is lexical.) There is, on the other hand, a fair amount of social variation in all three types. This variation may be described as involving—as far as pronunciation is concerned—'mild' and 'broad' accents. While all AusNZEng and SAfEng accents are phonologically very close to RP, phonetically there are differences: the 'mild' accents differ somewhat from RP, while the 'broad' accents differ considerably from RP. The 'mild' accents tend to be found towards the top of the social scale, particularly amongst older speakers. (RP is an accent which still has considerable prestige in these three countries, but there has been a very marked decline in this prestige in the last two decades or so.)

2.2.1   Australian and New Zealand English

2.2.1.1   AusEng Vowels: Phonological Differences from RP Vowels

1   Like south-of-England non-RP accents, AusEng has /iː/ rather than /ɪ/ in *very*, *many*, etc. Thus, *seedy* has the same vowel in both syllables in AusEng, while the vowels in *city* differ (see 2.1.2(1), page 11).

2   Like south-of-England non-RP accents, but to a much greater extent, AusEng has /ə/ rather than /ɪ/ in unstressed syllables. Thus, not only does /ə/ occur in the final syllable of *horses* and *wanted*, it also occurs in the final syllable of *naked*, *David*, *honest*, *village*, etc. (see 2.1.2(3), page 12). This applies also in the unstressed syllables in words such as *begin* /bəgɪn/ and *laxity* /læksətiː/.

3   AusEng follows RP in having /ɑː/ in *laugh*, *path*, *grass*, etc., but it differs from RP, and is more like non-RP north-of-England accents, in often having /æ/ in *dance*, *sample*, *plant*, *branch*, etc. (see 2.1.2(4), page 12). Pronunciations of the latter set with /ɑː/ do, however, occur: there is some regional variation in this (/ɑː/ is said to be especially common in South Australia) as well as variation from word to word. Other things being equal, /ɑː/ forms are considered somewhat more prestigious than /æ/ forms.

4   RP smoothing of /auə/ > /ɑ:/, etc., does not occur (see 2.1.1(2), page 11).

2.2.1.2   AusEng Vowels: Phonetic Differences from RP Vowels

Phonetic differences between RP and AusEng are considerable and, of course, most noticeable in 'broad' Australian accents. (In some respects AusEng pronunciation resembles that of the London area of England more than RP, but there are many dissimilarities also.) These phonetic differences are most obvious in the case of vowels, which are shown in table 2.3. Although we are concentrating in this book on varieties employed by more educated speakers, it is possible in the case of AusNZEng and SAfEng accents to give more information by illustrating those varieties most unlike RP—i.e., 'broad' accents. 'Milder' accents are then those that are intermediate between 'broad' accents and RP.

Table 2.3   *Phonetic Differences between Broad AusEng and RP Vowels* *

		RP	Broad AusEng
bid	/ɪ/	[ɪ]	[i̞]
bed	/ɛ/	[ɛ]	[e̞]
bad	/æ/	[æ]	[ɛ̞]
pot	/ɒ/	[ɒ]	[ɔ̞]
putt	/ʌ/	[ɐ]	[ɐ̈]
put	/ʊ/	[ʊ]	[ʊ]
bee	/i:/	[i̞i]	[ɜ·ɪ]
bay	/ei/	[eɪ]	[a̠·ɪ]
buy	/ai/	[aɪ]	[ɒ·ɪ] ~ [ɒ·ə]
boy	/ɔi/	[ɔɪ]	[o·ɪ]
boot	/u:/	[ɰu]	[ʉʉ̶]
boat	/ou/	[ɵu]	[ɒ·ʉ] ~ [ɐ·ə]
bout	/au/	[aʊ]	[æ·ʉ] ~ [æ·ɒ]
peer	/ɪə/	[ɪə]	[i̞·]
pair	/ɛə/	[ɛə]	[e̞:]
paw	/ɔ:/	[ɔ:]	[o:]
bard	/ɑ:/	[ɑ:]	[a:]
bird	/ɜ:/	[ɜ:]	[ə:]

* *The words in table 2.3 are also used in the recording for NZEng (see page 121).*

The distinctive differences shown in the table are:

1   AusEng front vowels tend to be closer than in RP (i.e. the body of the tongue is closer to the palate).
2   Some of the dipthongs are wider than in RP (i.e. the difference between the open first element and close second element is greater in AusEng than in RP).

3 There is a tendency for the diphthong to be 'slower', i.e. with a longer first element, than in RP, and even for diphthongs to become monophthongized, as in /ai/ as [ɒ·ɪ ~ ɒ·¹ ~ ɒ·ᵊ].
4 The /ɑː/ vowel is a very front [aː], in comparison to most other varieties of English.

2.2.1.3 AusEng Consonants

For AusEng consonants, we can note the following:

1 AusEng is non-rhotic and has linking and intrusive /r/ (see 2.1.3(4), page 13).
2 Intervocalic /t/ as in *city*, *better*, may become the voiced flap—[ḍ], as in NAmEng. However, this is by no means so common, standard, or consistent as it is in NAmEng, and [t] is also frequent in this environment. The glottal stop realization of /t/ may occur in *fit them*, as in RP, but not in any other environment. Glottal reinforcement as in *box*, *batch* does not occur (see 2.1.3(3), page 13).

2.2.1.4 Other AusEng Pronunciation Features

1 *Assume* etc. may be pronounced as /əšúːm/ rather than /əsúːm/ ~ /əsjúːm/. Similarly, *presume* etc. can have /ž/ rather than /z/ or /zj/.
2 In some areas, /ɔː/ may be heard in *off*, *often* etc. more frequently than in RP.
3 *Australia*, *auction*, *salt*, which may have /ɒ/ or /ɔː/ in RP, have only /ɒ/ in AusEng (see 2.1.1(3), page 11).
4 Days of the week tend to be pronounced with final /eɪ/ rather than RP /ɪ/ especially by younger speakers: *Monday* /mʌndeɪ/.
5 Initial /tj/, /dj/ may be pronounced as [č], [ǰ], e.g. *tune* [čə·ʉn], though this is not especially common in educated usage. (This feature is also found in many BritEng varieties.)

2.2.1.5 NZEng Pronunciation

Phonologically and phonetically NZEng accents are very similar to AusEng, and 'mild' AusEng and NZEng accents are very difficult for outsiders to tell apart, as the recording illustrates. The main differences between AusEng and NZEng pronunciation are the following:

1 In NZEng *dance*, *sample*, *grant*, *branch* etc. normally (but not always) have /ɑː/ (= [aː]) rather than /æ/. (*Telegraph*, *graph*, though, most usually have /æ/.)

2   The front vowels /æ/ as in *bad* and /ɛ/ as in *bed* tend to be even closer than in AusEng: *bad* [bɛd], *bed* [bed].

3   The vowel /ɪ/ as in *bid* is a central vowel in the region of [ɨ ~ ə], and the contrast between AusEng *bid* [bid] and NZEng [bəd] is very clear, cf. *Philip*: RP [fɪlɪp], AusEng [fɪləp], NZEng [fələp]. For very many New Zealanders there is thus no contrast between /ɪ/ and /ə/.

4   There is a strong tendency in NZEng for /ɪə/ and /ɛə/ to merge; thus *beer* and *bare* = [bẹ̈:].

5   The tendency towards monophthongization of /ai/, etc. is less strong than in AusEng.

6   NZEng /u:/ tends to be less diphthongal than in many AusEng varieties, thus [ʉ:] or even [ɨ:].

7   *Old, toll, sold* etc. may have /ɒ/ rather than /ou/—for many speakers /ɒ/ and /ou/ are neutralized before /l/.

8   In NZEng, the /ʍ/ of *which* appears to be retained more frequently than in AusEng, and possibly more than in RP.

9   NZEng is mainly non-rhotic, and has linking and intrusive /r/. In some locations settled originally by Scots, however, such as parts of Otago and Southland, rhotic forms may still be heard.

10   The word *with* may be pronounced /wɪθ/ (as in some NAmEng and ScotEng varieties) rather than /wɪð/.

11   Initial /kw/ is often pronounced /k/ in *quarter* /kɔ:tə/.

2.2.1.6   Grammatical Differences between AusNZEng and EngEng

At the level of educated speech and writing, there are very few obvious grammatical differences between AusNZEng and EngEng. It is, for example, usually not possible to tell if a text has been written by an English, Australian or New Zealand writer—unless by the vocabulary (see below). There are, however, a few distinctive tendencies:

1   The use of the auxiliaries *shall* and *should* with first-person subjects, as in *I shall go, We should like to see you*, is less usual in AusNZEng than in EngEng, and even in EngEng these are now increasingly replaced by *will* and *would*, as in *I will go/I'll go, We would like to see you*.

2   In EngEng, the following negative forms of *used to* are all possible:

   He used not to go
   He usedn't to go
   He didn't use to go

with the first (older and more formal) construction being the most usual in writing. In AusNZEng, the third form is less usual than in EngEng, while the second form is probably more usual than in

EngEng. Contracted forms without *to*—*He usedn't go*—are also more usual in AusNZEng than in EngEng.

3   For many speakers of EngEng, the auxiliary *do* is normally used in tag questions in sentences with the auxiliary *ought*: *He ought to go, didn't he?* In AusNZEng, *do* is not used in such cases; instead, *should* or *ought* would occur (i.e. *shouldn't he?*, *oughtn't he?* in the above sentence).

4   The occurrence of *do* with an auxiliary when *do* substitutes for a verb, as in *Are you going tonight? I may do/I could do/I should do*, which is quite normal in EngEng, is less common in AusNZEng (for fuller discussion of *do* substitution, see 4.1.1.3, page 51).

5   The use of *have* in expressing possession, as in *I have a new car*, is more usual in EngEng than in AusNZEng, where *got*, as in *I've got a new car*, is preferred.

6   EngEng permits all the following double-object constructions (with some regional variation):

I'll give it him
I'll give him it
I'll give it to him

The construction with *to* is probably the most frequent in EngEng, especially in the south of England, and it is this form which is the most usual in AusNZEng.

7   In EngEng it is quite usual for collective nouns to take plural verbs:

The government have made a mistake
The team are playing very badly

The reverse is the usual case in AusNZEng, where the above two sentences would tend to have the singular forms *has* and *is*, respectively (see also 4.1.2.2, page 58).

8   In colloquial AusEng, the feminine pronoun *she* can be used to refer to inanimate nouns and in impersonal constructions:

She'll be right ('Everything will be all right')
She's a stinker today ('The weather is excessively hot today').

2.2.1.7   Lexical Differences between EngEng and AusEng

Vocabulary differences between the Australasian varieties and EngEng are very small when compared to differences between the 'English' and 'American' varieties, hence the brevity of the word lists in this section. They are, however, numerous enough at the level of colloquial vocabulary. Some of the differences between EngEng and AusEng vocabulary are the result of borrowings into AusEng from Australian aboriginal languages. Well-known examples of such loans include *boomerang*, *dingo* (a wild dog), and *billabong* (a cut-off river channel), as well as many names for indigenous flora and fauna. In other cases the differences are purely intra-English. We give a short list of these below by way of illustration of types of lexical difference. Word lists consisting only of corresponding words in two dialects are often misleading, since differences can be quite subtle and may involve differences in frequency of use, style, or in only one particular sub-sense of a word. We therefore supplement the list with notes.

	AusEng	*EngEng*
1	*to barrack for*	*to support*
2	*bludger*	*a loafer, sponger*
3	*footpath*	*pavement*
4	*frock*	*dress*
5	*get*	*fetch*
6	*goodday*	*hello*
7	*gumboots*	*wellington boots*
8	*(one storey) house*	*bungalow*
9	*lolly*	*sweet*
10	*paddock*	*field*
11	*parka*	*anorak*
12	*picture theatre*	*cinema*
13	*radiator*	*(electric) fire*
14	*sedan*	*saloon car*
15	*singlet*	*vest*
16	*station*	*stock farm*
17	*station wagon*	*estate car*
18	*stove*	*cooker*
19	*stroller*	*push-chair*
20	*wreckers*	*breakers*

Notes

1 *To barrack for* is a term used for support at, e.g. football matches and of sports teams: *Who do you barrack for?* The term *to barrack* is known in EngEng but in the meaning of 'shouting abuse or unfavourable comments' at sports teams, and is now somewhat old-fashioned.

2 *Bludger* is colloquial only.

3 In EngEng, *footpath* refers to a path across fields, through woods, etc., while *pavement* refers to a pathway beside a road or street. In AusEng, *footpath* covers both. Both *pavement* and *sidewalk* do occur, however, in certain areas of Australia and New Zealand.

4 Both varieties permit both words. *Frock*, however, sounds old-fashioned in EngEng and is not used in advertising as it is in AusEng.

5 *Get* is widely used in both varieties, but usages such as *I'll fetch it*

for you are much less usual in AusEng than in EngEng.

6 *Goodday* [gədei] is a common, colloquial form of greeting in AusEng.

7 *Gumboots* is understood in EngEng but sounds rather archaic. Both varieties also use the term *rubber boots*.

8 EngEng distinguishes between *bungalow* 'a one-storey house' and *house* 'a two or more storey house', although *house* is also a generic term covering both. In Australia (where, in fact, bungalows are a good deal more common than in Britain), this distinction is not made. *Bungalow*, however, is used in AusEng to refer to a less substantial construction such as a summer house, beach bungalow, etc.

9 In EngEng, *lolly* is an abbreviation of *lollipop*, which is a sweet on a stick, designed for licking. In AusEng, *lolly* is a generic term corresponding to EngEng *sweet*. *Sweet* is used in AusEng, but usually as a rather formal shop-type word.

10 The word *paddock* is used in EngEng with the more restricted meaning of a field that is used for grazing horses. The AusEng usage refers to any piece of fenced-in land. *Field* is used in AusNZEng with abstract meaning and also in reference to, e.g. a *football field* (= EngEng *football pitch*). Many words referring to European-type countryside features, such as *brook*, *stream*, *meadow* are unusual or poetic in AusEng.

11 The word *parka* is known in EngEng but in recent years has been replaced by *anorak*, although some manufacturers may make a distinction, using these terms, between different types of coat. (Both words are loans from Eskimo.)

12 *Cinema* is in fact used in both varieties, but is rather higher style in AusEng. One doesn't say *picture theatre* in EngEng, but both varieties have the informal phrase *going to the pictures*.

13 *Radiator* is used in EngEng, but only with reference to hot water or oil radiators, e.g. those used in central-heating systems. In EngEng both portable and fixed heaters consisting of electrically heated bars are known as *fires*.

14 Here AusEng follows NAmEng.

15 The garment referred to here is an undershirt. *Singlet* is known and used in EngEng, but *vest* is not usual in AusEng.

16 In AusEng a *station* refers to a large cattle or sheep farm (besides having the meaning common to all forms of English, as in *railway station*).

17 Here AusEng follows NAmEng.

18 *Cooker* is not usual in AusEng, while both *cooker* and *stove* are used in EngEng.

19 *Stroller* is known in EngEng, but is not so widely used as *push-chair*. Some forms of AusNZEng also use *push-chair* or '*pushy*'.

20 The reference here is to premises dealing with old, broken down, or crashed cars.

Most lexical differences within the English-speaking world can be found at the level of colloquial speech, and especially in that faddish, often transitory form known as 'slang'. AusEng slang or colloquial expressions not known in EngEng include:

to chunder	'to vomit'
crook	'ill, angry'
dag	'amusing person'
dink	'a lift on a bicycle' (Melbourne only)
drongo or *nong*	'a fool'
to nick off	'to depart'
to rubbish	'to pour scorn on'
a Sheila	'a girl'
shickered	'drunk'
to sling off at	'to speak disparagingly to'
this arvo	'this afternoon'

Readers should be warned that slang, by its very nature, is liable (although not bound) to change with time, and that information of the above sort can very rapidly become out of date.

2.2.1.8 Lexical Differences between EngEng and NZEng

In most respects, NZEng vocabulary agrees either with AusEng (e.g. *lolly*) or with EngEng. NZEng usages include:

NZEng	*EngEng*
bach (North Island) ⎫	
crib (South Island) ⎬	*cabin, holiday cottage*
bowser	*petrol station*
pakeha (from Maori)	*white person*
tramping	*hiking*

Other more colloquial NZEng terms are:

gutzer	'a fall' (also used in AusEng—now old-fashioned)
joker	'bloke, fellow, guy'
puckeroo(ed)	'broken down' (from Maori)
school	'group of drinkers'
whare /wɒriː/	'small house or hut' (from Maori)

NZEng *hurray!* can function as a leave-taking formula (= *goodbye*) (also known in AusEng); and *good (thanks)* is a possible reply to *How are you?* (which is not possible in EngEng, where *fine, not bad, OK, very well, thank you*, etc. are usual).

2.2.2   South African English

Unlike in Australia and New Zealand, native English speakers do not form the majority of the population of South Africa. Out of a total population of around 22 million, native English speakers number less than 2½ million, and of these perhaps 1 million are genuinely bilingual in English and Afrikaans. (Of the rest of the population, about 15 million speak Bantu languages, and 3½ million speak Afrikaans. There are also sizeable communities of speakers of Indian and European languages.)

English resembling SAfEng is also spoken natively in Namibia (South West Africa), Zimbabwe, Zambia, Kenya and other areas of Southern and Eastern Africa.

2.2.2.1   SAfEng Vowels

As we have noted in the case of AusNZEng, as far as pronunciation is concerned there is a fair amount of variation in SAfEng ranging from RP or near RP to 'broad' SAfEng. A complicating factor in South Africa, however, is the influence of Afrikaans on English. (Obviously, native speakers of Afrikaans show intereference from their language when speaking English; but the influence of Afrikaans can also be found in the English of Afrikaans-English bilinguals and even in that of monolingual English speakers.) The English spoken natively and as a second language by the 'coloured' (i.e. mixed race) communities in South Africa also differs from that of whites in a number of respects.

SAfEng phonology is identical to that of many south-east England varieties, but its phonetics is perhaps closest to that of NZEng.

1   SAfEng differs from RP in having /i:/ in the last syllable of *very, many* etc. (as do AusNZEng).
2   As in AusNZEng, SAfEng has /ə/ in the unstressed syllable of *naked, village*, etc.
3   Like RP and NZEng (but unlike AusEng), SAfEng has /ɑ:/ in *dance*, etc. Note, however, that this is a distinctively back vowel (see table 2.4) and that it is this feature which most readily distinguishes between mild SAfEng and mild AusNZEng accents.
4   The distinction of allophones of /ɪ/ in SAfEng is quite complex. For instance, /ɪ/ = [ə] in *pin* [pən], but before /š/, /ɪ/ = [ɪ], *fish* [fɪš]. In Afrikaans-influenced speech, on the other hand, /ɪ/ = [i].

↓This makes little sense, since Afrikaans
/ɪ/ is [ə] (& /i/ is [i]).

5   In SAfEng, the tendency for diphthongs to be monophthongized is much stronger than in AusEng, at least in 'broad' varieties.

Table 2.4 shows the phonetic realization of vowels in one form of SAfEng. As with AusEng, we show a fairly 'broad' form of white SAfEng pronunciation.

Table 2.4   SAfEng Vowels

		RP	SAfEng
bid	/ɪ/	[ɪ]	[ə]
bed	/ɛ/	[ɛ]	[e]
bad	/æ/	[æ]	[ɛ]
pot	/ɒ/	[ɒ]	[ɔ]
putt	/ʌ/	[ɐ]	[ɐ˕]
put	/ʊ/	[ʊ]	[u]
bee	/iː/	[ɟi]	[iː]
bay	/ei/	[eɪ]	[ɐe]
buy	/ai/	[aɪ]	[ɑ·ə]
boy	/ɔi/	[ɔɪ]	[oe]
boot	/uː/	[ɥu]	[ʉː]
boat	/ou/	[ɵʊ]	[ʌ˕·ə]
bout	/au/	[aʊ]	[æ·ə]
peer	/ɪə/	[ɪə]	[eː]
pair	/ɛə/	[ɛə]	[eː]
paw	/ɔː/	[ɔː]	[oː]
bard	/aː/	[ɑː]	[ɒː]
bird	/ɜː/	[ɜː]	[ø˔ː]

2.2.2.2   SAfEng Consonants

1   There is a strong tendency, possibly as a result of Afrikaans influence, for /p/, /t/, /č/, /k/ to be unaspirated: *pin* RP [pʰɪn], SAfEng [pən].
2   As in AusNZEng, there is a tendency for intervocalic /t/, as in *better*, to be a voiced flap [d], although this is not so widespread or consistent as in NAmEng.
3   In a number of varieties of SAfEng, the 'dark *l*' [ɫ] allophone of /l/ as in *hill* does not occur (see 2.1.3(1), page 12).
4   SAfEng is *r*-less, lacking non-prevocalic *r* (except in Afrikaans-influenced English varieties). Very many varieties of SAfEng also lack both intrusive *r* and linking *r* (see 2.1.3(4), page 13): thus, *four o'clock* [foː(ʔ)əklɔk], *law and order* [loːŋoːdə]. SAfEng is alone among the 'English' varieties of English in having this characteristic.
There is a strong tendency for /r/ to be a flap [ɾ], unlike the

frictionless continuant [ɹ] of RP or AusNZEng. (Afrikaans speakers often use a trilled [r].)

5   /tj/, /dj/ often are realized as [č], [ǰ], as in many EngEng varieties: *tune* [čʉ:n] (cf. AusEng).

2.2.2.3   SAfEng Grammar

There appear to be even fewer grammatical differences between SAfEng and EngEng than between AusNZEng and EngEng, especially at the level of educated speech.

1   The EngEng construction with *do*-substitution after an auxiliary, as in *I might do, I should have done*, is not found very frequently in SAfEng (cf. 2.2.1.6 (4), page 20, and 4.1.1.3, page 51).

2   A common SAfEng feature is the use of the all-purpose response question *is it?*, invariable for person, tense or auxiliary, which corresponds to the complex series *do they, can't he, shouldn't we, will you*, etc. used in other varieties:

> *He's gone to town.—Oh, is it?* (= EngEng, *Oh, has he?*)

3   In 'broader' varieties of SAfEng it is possible in certain constructions and contexts to delete object noun phrases (NPs) after verbs which must have NPs in other varieties, e.g.:

> *Have you got?*
> *Have you sent?*
> *Did you put?*

4   Complement structures of *adjective + infinitive* occur where other varieties have *adjective + of + participle*:

> *This plastic is capable to withstand heat*
> (= This plastic is capable of withstanding heat)

5   Non-negative *no* occurs as an introductory particle:

> *How are you?*
> *No, I'm fine, thanks*

The force of this is often to negate assumptions made in the preceding question or comment.

2.2.2.4   SAfEng Lexis

As with AusNZEng, the contact of SAfEng with other languages has had an effect on its vocabulary. Among the better known borrowings are:

> *from Zulu:*
> *impi*   'African warrior band'
> *indaba*   'conference'
> *from Afrikaans:*
> *dorp*   'village'

kraal	'African village'
sjambok	'whip'
veld	'flat, open country'

Differences within formal English vocabulary are not especially numerous but include:

SAfEng	*EngEng*
bioscope	*cinema*
location	(Black) *ghetto*
reference book	*identity document*
robot	*traffic light*

2.3 Welsh English

Until quite recently, in most areas of Wales English was a second language learnt in school (as was the case in the Highlands of Scotland). Although this is no longer true and a majority of people in Wales are now native speakers of English, the effect is that Welsh English, at the level of educated speech and writing, is not much different from that of England, except phonetically and phonologically. There are, of course, distinctly Welsh lexical items and grammatical constructions, often due to the influence of Welsh, but Welsh Standard English cannot be said to be particularly different from EngEng. Most differences are found at the level of more localized dialects (see Wells (1982), and Hughes and Trudgill (1979)).

2.3.1 WEng Vowels

The Welsh English vowel system is, with some regional variation, as in table 2.5 (page 28) and on the recording.

The principal phonological differences between WEng and RP are the following:

1 *last, dance* etc. tend to have /æ/ rather than /ɑ:/ for most WEng speakers, though /ɑ:/ is found for many speakers in some words.
2 Unstressed orthographic *a* tends to be /æ/ rather than /ə/, e.g. *sofa* [soːfæ].
3 Unstressed orthographic *o* tends to be /ɒ/ rather than /ə/, e.g. *condemn* /kɒndɛm/.
4 There is no contrast between /ʌ/ and /ə/: *rubber* /rəbə/.
5 There is, in many varieties, an additional contrast, between /ei/ and /ɛi/:

made	/meid/	[meːd]
maid	/mɛid/	[mẹɪd]

Words with /ɛi/ are typically those spelt with *ai* or *ay*.

Table 2.5   WEng Vowels

/ɪ/	[ɪ]	*bid*
/ɛ/	[ɛ]	*bed*
/æ/	[a]	*bad, pass, ab̲ove, sofa̲*
/ɒ/	[ɔ]	*pot, ob̲ject* (v.)
/ʌ/	[ə]	*putt, famo̲u̲s, ru̲bber*
/ʊ/	[ʊ]	*put*
/iː/	[iː]	*bee*
/ei/	[eː]	*bake*
/ai/	[əɪ]	*buy*
/ɔi/	[ɔɪ]	*boy*
/uː/	[uː]	*boot*
/ou/	[oː]	*boat, board*
/ɑu/	[əʊ]	*bout*
/ɛə/	[ɛː]	*pair*
/ɔː/	[ɔː]	*sort, paw*
/ɑː/	[aː]	*bard, calm*
/ɜː/	[øː]	*bird*
/ɛi/	[ɛ̧ɪ]	*bait*
/ɔu/	[ɔ̧ʊ]	*blow*

6   There is, in many varieties, an additional contrast between /ou/ and /ɔu/:

nose	/nouz/	[noːz]
knows	/nɔuz/	[nɔ̧ʊz]

7   Many words which have /ɔː/ in RP have, in many WEng varieties, the vowel /ou/ = [oː]. Thus:

	RP	*WEng*
so	[sɵu]	[soː]
soar	[sɔː]	[soː]

Note, however, that *port, paw* still have /ɔː/ in WEng.

8   The vowels /ɪə/, /ʊə/ do not occur in many varieties of WEng. *Fear* is /fiːjə/, *poor* is /puːwə/. Similarly, *fire* is /faijə/.

9   Words such as *tune, music* have /tɪʊn/, /mɪʊzɪk/ rather than /tjuːn/, /mjuːzɪk/.

2.3.2   WEng Consonants

1   Educated WEng is, with a few exceptions in the east and far south-west of the country, not rhotic; and intrusive and linking /r/ do occur; /r/ is often a flapped [ɾ].

2   Voiceless plosives tend to be strongly aspirated, and in word-final position are generally released and without glottalisation, e.g. *pit* [pʰɪtʰ].

3 /l/ is clear [l] in all positions.
4 There is a strong tendency for intervocalic consonants to be lengthened before unstressed syllables:

> *butter*   [bətʰ:ə]
> *money*   [mən:i]

5 The Welsh consonants /ɬ/ and /x/ occur in place-names and loan-words from Welsh. (/ɬ/ is a voiceless, lateral fricative, and /x/ is a voiceless velar fricative as in Scots *loch* or German *acht*), e.g.:

> *Llanberis*   /ɬanbɛ́rɪs/
> *bach*   /bɑːx/ (term of endearment)

2.3.3 Non-systematic Pronunciation Differences

1 For some WEng speakers, /g/ is absent in the following two words:

	WEng	**RP**
language	/læŋwɛ̌ǰ/	/læŋgwɪ̌ǰ/
longer	/lɒŋə/	/lɑŋgə/

2 For some WEng speakers, /ʊ/ occurs in both of the following words:

	WEng	**RP**
comb	/kʊm/	/koum/
tooth	/tʊθ/	/tuːθ/

2.3.4 WEng Grammar

The following features can be observed in the speech of even some educated WEng speakers, but are not usually encountered in written Welsh English:

1 The use of the universal tag question *isn't it?*, invariable for main clause person, tense or auxiliary:
> *You're going now, isn't it?* (= EngEng: *aren't you?*)
> *They do a lot of work, isn't it?* (= EngEng: *don't they?*)
2 The use of *will* for *will be*:
> *Is he ready? No, but he will in a minute.*
3 The use of predicate object inversion for emphasis:
> WEng: *Coming home tomorrow he is*
> EngEng: *He's coming home tomorrow/It's tomorrow he's coming home*
4 The use of negative *too*:
> WEng: *I can't do that, too*
> EngEng: *I can't do that, either*

5   The use of adjective and adverb reduplication for emphasis:
   WEng: *It was high, high*
   EngEng: *It was very high*

2.3.5   WEng Lexis

Surprisingly few Welsh loan-words are used in standard WEng.
Common words include:

del	/dɛl/	a term of endearment
eisteddfod	/aistɛðvɒd/	a competitive arts festival (This word is known to EngEng speakers, who generally pronounce it /aistɛðfəd/.)
llymru	/ɬəmriː/	porridge dish

   Different WEng usages of English words found in some parts of
Wales include:

delight	'interest'	(e.g. 'a delight in languages')
rise	'get, buy'	(e.g. 'I'll rise the drinks')
tidy	'good, nice'	(e.g. 'a tidy car')

Again, most vocabulary differences are at the level of non-standard
or colloquial usage.

3
The Pronunciation of North American English

The sociolinguistic situation in the United States and Canada, as far as pronunciation is concerned, is rather different from that of the rest of the English-speaking world. There is more regional variation in NAm pronunciation than in AusNZEng and SAfEng, yet there is no universally accepted totally regionless standard pronunciation as in EngEng.

In this chapter we will begin by giving an outline of one USEng accent—an accent employed by some educated white middle-class speakers from the central east-coast region. We will then point to differences between this accent and RP. Next we will discuss regional differences within NAmEng pronunciation, concentrating on varieties of educated speech and omitting mention of most lower-prestige and/or localized accents.

3.1 North American English Vowels

*Table 3.1   USEng Vowel System (Central East Coast)**

/ɪ/	bid, mirror, wanted
/ɛ/	bed, merry
/æ/	bad, marry, path, dance, half, banana
/ɑ/	pot, bard, father, calm, horrid
/ʌ/	putt, hurry
/ʊ/	put
/i/	bee, very, peer
/ei/	bay, pair, Mary
/ai/	buy, fire, night, ride
/ɔi/	boy
/u/	boot, tour
/ou/	boat
/ɑu/	bout, loud, tower
/ɔ/	paw, port, talk, boring, long, pore
/ə/	about, sofa, bird, furry, butter

* The words in table 3.1 are also used in the recording for USEng (Mid-Western) and CanEng (see page 121).

Table 3.1 and the first US speaker on the recording illustrate the vowel system of the USEng accent described above. Note that, to aid comparison, vowel symbols have been chosen which are closest to those used in chapter 2 for the 'English' type accents rather than those typically used by American writers. Note also that this phonological analysis is not so widely accepted as the analysis of RP vowels given in 2.1.1 (page 10). In particular, the identification of vowel phonemes before /r/ (especially the vowels of *bird, port* and *furry*) is not entirely uncontroversial in view of the considerable allophonic variation before /r/ : /i/—*peer* [pɪəɹ]; /ei/—*pair* [pɛəɹ]; /ai/—*fire* [faɪəɹ]; /u/—*tour* [tʊəɹ]; /au/—*tower* [taʊəɹ]; /ɔ/—*port* [pɔəɹt]; /ə/—*bird* [bə:ɹd] ~ [bɹ̩d] . This allophonic variation is particularly clear on the recording.

3.1.1 NAmEng Vowels: Phonological Differences from RP

1 NAmEng agrees with all other English varieties we have discussed in differing from RP by having /i/ rather than /ɪ/ in *very*, etc. (However, a number of south-eastern and eastern USA varieties *do* have /ɪ/ here.)
2 The three RP vowels /ɒ/, /æ/ and /ɑ:/ correspond to only two vowels in NAmEng—/ɑ/ and /æ/. This, combined with the phonetic difference between RP /ɒ/ and USEng /ɑ/ and a difference in vowel distribution in many sets of words, makes for a complicated set of correspondences. When this is further combined with a different distribution in word sets of the vowels /ɑ/ and /ɔ/ (NAm): /ɒ/ and /ɔ:/ (RP) and the rhotic/non-rhotic difference, the picture becomes even more complex:

	RP	NAmEng
bad	æ	æ
Datsun	æ	ɑ
Bogota	ɒ	ou
pot	ɒ	ɑ
cough	ɒ	ɔ
long	ɒ	ɔ̇
paw	ɔ:	ɔ
port	ɔ:	ɔr
bard	ɑ:	ɑr
path	ɑ:	æ
dance	ɑ:	æ
half	ɑ:	æ
banana	ɑ:	æ
father	ɑ:	ɑ

This chart illustrates the following points:

(a) In very many words spelled with *a*, the correspondence is straightforward: in *cat, bad, man,* etc. RP /æ/ = NAmEng /æ/. Similarly, in very many words spelled with *o*, the correspondence is also reliable: in *pot, top, nod,* etc. RP /ɒ/ = NAmEng /ɑ/.

The remaining points are somewhat problematic:

(b) Perhaps because in many varieties of NAmEng /æ/ tends to be rather closer than in RP (see below), many words felt to be 'foreign' have /ɑ/ in NAmEng corresponding to the /æ/ in RP. Thus *Milan* is /mɪlǽn/ in RP but may be /mɪlάn/ in NAmEng, and *Datsun* in NAmEng is /dάtsn̩/, as if it were spelled *Dotsun*. This tendency is not entirely uncomplicated, however, as there are some words, e.g. *khaki,* where the reverse correspondence is found, i.e. USEng /kǽki/, RP /kɑ:kɪ/. (CanEng often has /karki/).

(c) Probably as a consequence of the fact that NAmEng /ɑ/ in *pot* is an unrounded vowel, 'foreign' words spelled with *o* tend to have /ou/ in NAmEng corresponding to /ɒ/ in EngEng:

	EngEng	*NAmEng*
Bogota	/bɒgəta:/	/bougəta/
Carlos	/ka:lɒs/	/karlous/

(d) NAmEng does not have the RP distinction /ɒ/—/ɑ:/ *bomb*—*balm*, and therefore has /ɑ/ not only in the set *pot, top,* but also for many words that have /ɑ:/ in RP including *father, calm* (for many speakers), *rather* (for some speakers). Thus *father* rhymes with *bother,* and *bomb* and *balm* are pronounced the same (but see 3.3(9), page 38).

(e) While both RP and the variety of NAmEng described here have a different vowel in *cot* than in *caught*—RP /kɒt/, /kɔ:t/: NAmEng /kɑt/, /kɔt/—the distribution of words over these vowels differs somewhat. In some cases RP /ɒ/ corresponds to NAm /ɑ/, and RP /ɔ:/ to NAm /ɔ/. But it is also the case that RP /ɒ/ corresponds to NAm /ɔ/ in words having an *o* before *ng* and in words having an *o* before one of the voiceless fricatives /f/, /θ/, /s/ (cf. 2.1.1 (3), page 11). In some areas this also applies to *o* before *g* as in *dog, fog.* This is illustrated in table 3.2 (page 34). Foreign learners may find the distribution of /ɑ/ and /ɔ/ in USEng confusing and hard to learn. They can take comfort, however, from the fact that many NAmEng accents in fact do not distinguish between these two vowels (see 3.3 below).

(f) While RP does not distinguish between *gnaw* and *nor*, NAmEng (being rhotic) does. (See *paw, port,* on chart.)

Table 3.2 *Word Distribution of* /ɒ/—/ɑ/ *and* /ɔː/—/ɔ/

RP /ɒ/	NAmEng /ɑ/	RP /ɔː/	NAmEng /ɔ/
cot	cot		
top	top		
pot	pot		
pond	pond		
	calm		
	father		
	Milan		
		caught	caught
		taught	taught
		launch	launch
		bought	bought
		all	all
		tall	tall
		saw	saw
loss			loss
cross			cross
soft			soft
cough			cough
off			off
cloth			cloth
song			song
long			long
wrong			wrong

(g) Being rhotic, NAmEng has /r/ in *bard* etc.. Note that the lack of the RP /ɒ/—/ɑː/ distinction means that *cod* /kad/ and *card* /kard/ are distinguished only by means of the /r/ (cf. RP *cod* /kɒd/, *card* /kɑːd/). However, *starry* and *sorry* are perfect rhymes: NAmEng /stari/—/sari/; EngEng /stɑːrɪ/—/sɒrɪ/.

(h) In words such as *path*, *laugh*, *grass*, where RP (but not northern English accents) has /ɑː/ before /θ/, /f/, /s/, NAmEng has /æ/.

(i) This applies also to RP /ɑː/ before /nt/, /ns/, /nč/, /nd/, /mp/. Thus NAmEng agrees with northern English accents and many types of AusEng in having /æ/ rather than /ɑː/ in *plant*, *dance*, *branch*, *sample*, etc.

(j) NAmEng, in this case unlike northern English accents, also has /æ/ in *half*, *banana*, *can't*.

3 NAmEng is a rhotic accent, with non-prevocalic /r/. This has the consequence that the following RP vowels (derived historically from vowel + /r/) do not occur in NAmEng:

/ɪə/ in *dear* (corresponds to NAm /ir/)
/ɛə/ in *dare* (corresponds to NAm /eɪr/)

/ʊə/ in *tour* (corresponds to NAm /ur/)
/ɜ:/ in *bird* (corresponds to NAm /ər/—but see 3.1 above)
(The final syllable in *idea*—identical in RP to the /ɪə/ of *peer, dear*—is
best regarded as being /i/ + /ə/ in NAmEng.)

3.1.2 NAmEng Vowels: Phonetic Differences from RP

Perhaps all vowels in NAmEng are somewhat different from RP
vowels. The major differences, however, are:

1 The vowel of *pot* is unrounded [ɑ] in NAmEng, rounded [ɒ] in
RP.
2 The vowel /ɔ/ of *paw* in USEng tends to be shorter, more open and
less rounded than the equivalent vowel /ɔ:/ in RP.
3 Very front realizations of /ou/ such as RP [øʉ] are not found in
most varieties of NAmEng, a typical NAmEng pronunciation being
[oʊ].
4 The diphthong /ei/ may be closer in NAmEng, [eɪ] as opposed to
RP [ɐ̞ɪ].
5 The first element of /au/ tends to be more front in NAmEng than
in RP: NAmEng [aʊ], RP [ɑʊ].

3.2 North American English Consonants

1 Glottal reinforcement as found in RP (see 2.1.3 (3b), page 13) is
not found in NAmEng. Neither is [ʔ] found as an allophone of /t/ in
most NAmEng varieties, except before /n/: *button* [bəʔn̩]; or, in New
York City and Boston, /l/: *bottle* [bɑʔl̩]. Final /t/, however, is often
unreleased in NAmEng, especially before a following consonant, as
in *that man*.
2 The RP allophonic differentiation of /l/: [l] vs. [ɫ] (see 2.1.3(1),
page 12) is either not found or not so strong in NAmEng. In most
varieties, /l/ is fairly dark in all positions.
3 Intervocalic /t/, as in *better*, in NAmEng is most normally a
vocalic flap [d̮], not unlike the flapped /r/, [ɾ], of some northern
British varieties of English (though not identical with it). In many
varieties the result is a neutralization of the distribution between /t/
and /d/ in this position, i.e. *ladder* and *latter* both have [d̮]. While the
intervocalic consonants are identical, in some varieties the original
distinction is preserved through vowel length, with the vowel before
/d/ being longer: *ladder* [læ·d̮ɹ], *latter* [læd̮ɹ]. In other varieties the
distinction may be marginally preserved as /d/ = [d], /t/ = [d̮].
    This flapped [d̮] is consistently used in NAmEng in *latter, city*, etc.
by most speakers, except in very formal styles, where [t] may occur. In

the suffix *-ity*, [d̯] may vary with [t], as in *obscurity, electricity*. In *plenty, twenty*, etc. [nt] alternates with [n ~ n̩ ~ nd]. Thus *winner* and *winter* may or may not be identical.

4   As we have noted, NAmEng is rhotic and has /r/ in *bird, card, car*, etc. (and in the word *colonel* [kɹn̩ɫ]). Phonetically speaking, too, the /r/ is pronounced rather differently from that of RP. Acoustically the impression is one of greater retroflexion (the tip of the tongue is curled back further) than in RP but in fact many Americans achieve this effect by the humping up of the body of the tongue rather than by actual retroflexion.

3.3 Variation within North American English

The NAmEng accent we have discussed so far is that of an educated central-eastern variety. Elsewhere in the eastern USA there are distinctive varieties to be found in New England, New York City, and the South-East (with certain south-eastern features extending as far west as Texas). In the rest of the USA and Canada, stretching all the way from New York State to the West Coast, variation in educated speech is, at the phonological level, very slight. Regional variation involves the following features:

1   Very many NAmEng accents, particularly those from the Mid-West and Canada, demonstrate a series of vowel mergers before /r/ in polysyllabic words—unlike the accent described above. Thus:
(a) /iː/ and /ɪ/ are not distinguished before /r/. This means that the vowel in *peer* and the initial syllable in *irritate* are identical, and *mirror* and *nearer* are perfect rhymes. The actual quality of the vowels in these cases is around [ɪ·].
(b) /ɛ/, /ei/ and /æ/ are not distinguished before /r/. Thus *merry*, *Mary* and *marry* are all identical. (Some NAmEng accents merge *merry* and *Mary*, but keep *marry* distinct.) The vowel in this case is around [ɛ·].
(c) /ə/ and /ʌ/ are not distinguished before /r/. Thus *hurry* and *furry* are perfect rhymes. The vowel in this case is around [əɹ ~ ɹ̩]. (In these accents it probably makes no sense to distinguish phonologically between /ə/ and /ʌ/: we can write /ə/ for *putt* and *about* as well as for *bird, furry, hurry*. These mergers can be clearly heard from the Mid-West speaker on the recording.)
2   In the vowel table given in 3.1 (page 31), we have shown *cot* /kɑt/ and *caught* /kɔt/ as distinct and indicated that *pore, port* have the

same vowel /ɔ/ as *caught*. In this eastern accent, moreover, words such as *horrible, forest, correspond, Florida* have /ɑ/, as in *cot*.

In many areas of the USA and Canada away from the East Coast and South-East, however, words in the *horrible* set have /ɔ/ rather than /ɑ/. In these areas, *hoary* and *horrid* have the same initial syllable, with /ɔ/. (Note that even in these areas *borrow, tomorrow, sorry*, have /ɑ/, except in Canada.) Alternatively, as for example in large areas of Illinois, both the set of *port, pore* and the set of *horrible* have /ou/. Thus *poke* /pouk/ = [pouk] and *pork* /pourk/ = [po·ᵊɪk].

3   It will be observed that in the neutral eastern accent outlined above, the following vowels can occur before /r/: /ɪ/, /ɛ/, /æ/, /ʌ/ (these in polysyllables only, as in *mirror, merry, marry, hurry*); and /ɑ/ *bard*, /i/ *peer*, /ei/ *pair*, /ai/ *fire*, /u/ *tour*, /au/ *tower*, /ɔ/ *port*, /ə/ *bird* (and /ɔi/ in *coir*, if this word is ever used). This leaves /ʊ/ and /ou/ as the only vowels not possible before /r/ (or in Illinois-type accents, /ʊ/ and /ɔ/). In fact, in some accents, particularly in the American South-East, pairs of words such as *hoarse* and *horse, mourning* and *morning, four* and *for*, which are identical elsewhere, are distinguished: *hoarse* /hours/, *horse* /hɔrs/. Thus /ʊ/ remains the sole vowel not occurring before /r/.

4   In large areas of the USA (particularly in the North and West) and in most of Canada, the distinction between /ɑ/ and /ɔ/ is absent or is currently being lost. This means that pairs such as *cot/caught*, *not/nought* are not distinguished, the vowel in both sets (in most cases) being around [ɑ]. (Even in many accents where the distinction is preserved, the phonetic difference between /ɑ/ and /ɔ/ is very small, perhaps [ɑ̡] as opposed to [ɒ̡]). In most of the accents which have this merger, pairs such as *par* and *pore, part* and *port* nevertheless remain distinct. In these cases, many phonologists regard the vowel of *port* [po·ᵊɪt] as being an allophone of /ou/ as in *boat* (cf. (2) above).

To summarize:

	RP	Eastern USA	USA West A	USA West B	USA West C	Canada
cot	/ɒ/	/ɑ/	/ɑ/	/ɑ/	/ɑ/	/ɑ/
caught	/ɔ:/	/ɔ/	/ɔ/	/ɔ/	/ɑ/	/ɑ/
port	/ɔ:/	/ɔr/	/ɔr/	/our/	/our/	/our/
horrid	/ɒ/	/ɑr/	/ɔr/	/our/	/our/	/our/
borrow	/ɒ/	/ɑr/	/ɑr/	/ɑr/	/ɑr/	/our/

The terms 'USA West A, B and C' are used here simply as labels for three different non-eastern systems with reference to these vowels and do not refer to specific unified geographical regions. Accents using the systems of USA West A, B and C are, however, found in western

Ohio, northern Illinois and southern Illinois, respectively.

5   In many areas of the southern USA there is no distinction between /ɪ/ and /ɛ/ before nasal consonants. Thus, while *pit* and *pet* are different, pairs such as *pin* and *pen* are pronounced the same, either with [ɪ] or with a vowel intermediate between [ɪ] and [ɛ].

6   In most varieties of NAmEng, again with the exception of parts of the American East and South, words such as *new, nude, tune, student, duke, due*, which in English RP have /nju-/, /tju-/ or /dju-/, have no /j/ (cf. 2.1.1(7), page 11): *tune* /tuːn/, *duke* /duːk/. Some areas of central Canada, however, have /tj/ and /dj/ as [č], [ǰ] (see 2.2.1.4 (5) page 18).

7   Although we have described NAmEng as rhotic, there are three main areas of which this is not true (although in all of these three areas rhotic forms appear currently to be on the increase, forms with non-prevocalic /r/ tending to be regarded as 'correct' or prestigious by many Americans). These three areas are:

(a) Eastern New England (and some maritime areas of Canada), including the city of Boston. In this area, both linking and intrusive /r/ are found (see 2.1.3(4), page 13). Here *shot* may not be distinct from *short*.

(b) New York City and a few immediately adjoining suburbs. Linking /r/ is usual here but intrusive /r/ is not especially common. Younger speakers are increasingly rhotic. Non-rhotic New York speech has no distinction between *part* and *pot*, *guard* and *god*. This is also true of the western part of area (a), e.g. Rhode Island. *Shot* and *short* are distinguished as /šɑt/ and /šɔt/.

(c) The South, especially the eastern parts of Virginia, north and south Carolina and Georgia. In this area, intrusive /r/ does not occur, and even lack of linking /r/ is not uncommon.

Note that, particularly in areas (a) and (b), there is a strong tendency for /r/ to be preserved after the vowel of *her, bird* (unlike RP).

8   In one respect the accent used in Boston and immediately adjoining areas resembles RP more closely than that of other NAm varieties. Boston has a relatively rounded /ɒ/ in *pot, hot* etc. and an unrounded vowel /a/ in *part, car* etc. (with no /r/, of course). This latter vowel is also used in words such as *path, dance, last* which have /æ/ in other NAmEng varieties but /ɑː/ in English RP. (The set of words which has /a/ rather than /æ/ in Boston is, however, not quite identical with the RP /ɑː/ set.) This system is currently in a state of flux among younger Bostonians as a result of influence from other NAmEng varieties.

9   We indicated above that most Americans have no distinction between *bomb* and *balm*, and that *bother* and *father* are perfect rhymes. In fact, in certain (particularly eastern) accents there *is* a distinction, with *balm* and *father* etc. having an additional, longer

vowel: *bomb* /bɑm/, *balm* /bɑːm/. This can be heard from the eastern speaker on the recording.

10 There is considerable variation in NAmEng in the pronunciation of the vowel /æ/. In particular, there is a strong, and fairly recent, tendency for this vowel to become much closer in northern cities such as Chicago, Detroit, Cleveland, Buffalo, Rochester and New York. This tendency is most obvious in the speech of younger speakers and is more common in some phonological environments (e.g. before certain consonants) than in others. Thus, *bad* may range from [bæ·d] through [bɛ·d] to [beəd] and even [bɪəd]. This change is accompanied by a corresponding fronting of the vowel /ɑ/ of *hot*, which may range from [hɑt] through [hat] even to [hæt].

11 A distinctively southern feature of USEng is the tendency to monophthongize /ai/. Thus: *high* [ha·], *ride* [ra·d].

12 Also found in many parts of the South is the diphthongization of, in particular, /ɪ/, /ə/, and /æ/, sometimes extending even so far as *bid* [bijəd], *bed* [bejəd], *bad* [bæijəd]. Other vowels may also participate in this process e.g. *on* [ɔʏn].

13 A further widespread south-eastern feature is the use of wide diphthongized pronunciations of /ei/, e.g. as [æɪ] and /ou/, e.g. as [ɐʊ] or [œʉ].

14 As far as pronunciation is concerned, a majority of Black speakers in the USA have accents which resemble, although they are by no means identical to, those of White southerners. Typical of educated Black speech throughout the USA for example, is the merger of the vowels of *pin* and *pen* and the absence of non-prevocalic and linking /r/.

15 A distinctively Canadian feature is one known as 'Canadian raising'. Although something similar is found in some southern varieties of USEng, in the north it appears to stop at the Canadian-American border. It is found in nearly all parts of Canada, with the exception of parts of the East coast. The feature involves the occurrence of very different allophones of /ai/ and /au/ depending on whether or not there is a following voiceless consonant. Thus:

/au/	*house*	[həus]	*houses*	[hauzəz]
	lout	[ləut]	*loud*	[laud]
/ai/	*knife*	[nəɪf]	*knives*	[naɪvz]
	tight	[təɪt]	*tide*	[taɪd]

Americans are often led by this to claim that Canadians say 'oot' (*out*). Canadian raising can be heard on the recording in *night*, *bout* and *about*.

3.4 Non-systematic Differences between North American English and English English Pronunciation

Many of the differences between 'American' and 'English' varieties of English involve the pronunciation of individual or small groups of words. We now give some indication of these.

1   We list first a few individual words which differ in no particularly predictable way between USEng and EngEng (note that CanEng often uses the EngEng variant; stress is the same for both pronunciations of these words):

	USEng	EngEng
charade	/šəreɪd/	/šərɑːd/
cordial	/kɔrjəl/	/kɔːdiːəl/
deterrant	/dɪtərənt/	/dɪtɛrənt/
herb	/ərb/	/hɜːb/
leisure	/ližər/	/lɛžə/ (also US)
lever	/lɛvər/	/liːvə/ (also US)
privacy	/praivəsi/	/prɪvəsɪ/ ~ /praivəsɪ/
route	/rut/ ~ /rɑut/	/ruːt/
schedule	/skɛjəl/	/šɛjuːl/
shone	/šoun/	/šɒn/
tomato	/təmeitou/	/təmɑːtou/
vase	/veis/ ~ /veiz/	/vɑːz/

2   NAmEng *aluminum* /əlúmənəm/ differs both in pronunciation and (as a reflection of this) in spelling from EngEng *aluminium* /ǽluːmínjəm/.

3   *Either*, *neither* can have either /iː/ː/i/ or /ai/ on both sides of the Atlantic, but in educated speech /iðər/ is more common in NAmEng, /aiðə/ in EngEng.

4   A number of words spelled with *er* have /ər/ in NAmEng corresponding to /ɑː/ ~ /ɑr/ elsewhere: *clerk*, NAmEng /klərk/, EngEng /klɑːk/. Similarly *derby*, *Berkshire*.

5   *Of*, *what*, *was* have /ʌ/ in NAmEng, /ɒ/ elsewhere. Thus *what* rhymes with *but* in NAmEng but with *not* in EngEng.

6   *Apparatus*, *data*, *status* can be pronounced with either stressed /æ/ or /ei/ in NAmEng, but only with stressed /ei/ in EngEng.

7   Words like *fertile*, *hostile*, *juvenile*, *missile*, *mobile*, *reptile*, *sterile* have final /ail/ in EngEng. In NAmEng, the final syllable may be either /ail/ or /əl/. Note that *docile* is /dousail/ in EngEng, /dɑsəl/ in NAmEng.

8   The prefixes *anti-* and *semi-* have final /ɪ/ ~ /iː/ in EngEng. In

addition to these pronunciations NAmEng also has final /ai/ for these prefixes.

9 *Tunisia* is pronounced /tunížə/ in NAmEng but /tju:nízi:ə/ in EngEng. *Asia* has /ž/ in NAmEng, /š/ or /ž/ in EngEng.

3.5 Stress Differences

1 In a number of words of foreign, especially French, origin, NAmEng tends to have stress on the final syllable while EngEng does not. Thus:

	NAmEng	*EngEng*
attaché	/ætæšéi/	/ətǽšei/
ballet	/bæléi/	/bǽlei/
baton	/bətán/	/bǽtɒn/
beret	/bəréi/	/bɛ́rɪ/ ~ /bɛ́rei/
debris	/dəbrí/	/dɛ́bri:/

2 There are a number of words having first-syllable stress in NAmEng but with stress elsewhere in EngEng. A few examples are:

	NAmEng	*EngEng*
address	/ǽdres/ ~ /ədrɛ́s/	/ədrɛ́s/
adult	/ǽdʌlt/ ~ /ǽdəlt/	/ədʌ́lt/ ~ /ǽdʌlt/
cigarette	/sígərɛt/ ~ /sɪgərɛ́t/	/sɪgərɛ́t/
inquiry	/íŋkwərɪ/ ~ /ɪŋkwáirɪ/	/ɪŋkwáiərɪ/
magazine	/mǽgəzin/ ~ /mægəzín/	/mǽgəzí:n/
margarine	/márǰərən/	/mɑ:ǰərí:n/
research	/rísərč/	/rəsɛ́:č/

Note that *research*, as a noun, is now increasingly pronounced with first-syllable stress in EngEng.

3 A number of compound words have acquired stress on the first element in NAmEng but retain stress on the second element in EngEng. These compounds include: *weekend*, *hotdog*, *New Year*, *icecream*.

4 Many polysyllabic words ending in *-ory* or *-ary* normally have stress on the first or second syllable in EngEng, with the penultimate syllable being reduced. In NAmEng there is, in addition, secondary stress on the penultimate syllable:

	NAmEng	*EngEng*
auditory	/ɔ́dɪtɔ̀ri/	/ɔ́:dɪtrɪ/
commentary	/káməntɛ̀ri/	/kɒ́məntrɪ/
dictionary	/díkšənɛ̀ri/	/díkšənrɪ/
lavatory	/lǽvətɔ̀ri/	/lǽvətrɪ/
secretary	/sékrətɛ̀ri/	/sékrətrɪ/

In EngEng, partially reduced pronunciations are also possible, but there is never secondary stress on the penultimate syllable: *dictionary* /díkšǝnǝrɪ/.

In a number of words of this set, the primary stress is also located differently:

	USEng	*EngEng*
laboratory	/lǽbrǝtɔ̀rɪ/	/lǝbɒ́rǝtrɪ/
corollary	/kárǝlɛ̀ri/	/kǝrɒ́lǝrɪ/
capillary	/kǽpɪlɛ̀ri/	/kǝpílǝrɪ/
ancillary	/ǽnsɪlɛ̀ri/	/ænsílǝrɪ/

(Note that all words discussed here have at least four syllables in NAmEng: i.e. none of the above remarks applies to, e.g. *vagary*.)

The same type of difference also appears in a number of words ending in *-mony*:

	NAmEng	*EngEng*
matrimony	/mǽtrɪmòuni/	/mǽtrɪmǝnɪ/
testimony	/tέstɪmòuni/	/tέstɪmǝnɪ/

5   Many place names (and family names derived from them) demonstrate more stress and vowel reduction in EngEng than in NAmEng:

	NAmEng	*EngEng*
Birmingham	/bɔ̀rmiŋhæ̀m/	/bɔ́ːmɪŋǝm/
Cunningham	/kʌ́nɪŋhæ̀m/	/kʌ̀nɪŋǝm/
Norfolk	/nɔ́rfouk/	/nɔ́ːfǝk/
Norwich	/nɔ́rwič/	/nɒ́rɪǰ/
Portsmouth	/pɔ́rtsmòuθ/	/pɔ́ːtsmǝθ/

3.6 Differences between American English and Canadian English Pronunciation

In a few respects Canadian pronunciation follows EngEng rather than USEng:

1   *been* is usually /bɪn/ in USEng, but occasionally /biːn/ in CanEng as, more usually, in EngEng.

2   *again(st)* is usually /ǝgέn/ in USEng. This pronunciation is also used in Canada and the UK, but in CanEng and EngEng it can also be /ǝgeín/.

3   As mentioned above, *corollary*, *capillary* are stressed on the first syllable in USEng, with secondary stress on the penultimate syllable. CanEng follows EngEng in having the stress on the second syllable.

4

English and North American English: Grammatical, Orthographical and Lexical Differences

At the level of educated speech and writing, there are relatively few differences in grammar and spelling between EngEng and NAmEng; those which do exist tend to be fairly trivial when considered from the point of view of mutual understanding. Vocabulary differences, on the other hand, are very numerous and are capable of causing varying degrees of comprehension problems. Each of these three areas will be discussed in turn below.

It should be noted that we treat EngEng and NAmEng, often, as if they were two entirely homogeneous and separate varieties. This makes the presentation of the facts more straightforward, but it does obscure, to a certain extent, the fact that there is regional variation, even in Standard English, in the two areas. There is also considerable influence of the one variety on the other, particularly of NAmEng on EngEng; thus, what is NAmEng usage for older English people may be perfectly normal EngEng usage for younger English people.

4.1 Grammatical Differences

In this section we will discuss differences both in morphology and syntax. We will also note some differences in frequency of use of certain constructions which occur in both varieties.

4.1.1 The Verb

4.1.1.1 Morphology

1 *Inflectional.* In English, 'regular' verbs are characterized as having two distinct 'principle parts': a present tense form, and a past tense/past participle form which is made by adding -*(e)d* to the present tense form, e.g.:

Present	Past	Past Participle
call	called	called
create	created	created

There are many 'irregular' or 'strong' verbs in English, however, which do not follow this pattern, diverging in a variety of ways: e.g.

Present	Past	Past Participle
fly	flew	flown
hit	hit	hit
sing	sang	sung
teach	taught	taught

In NAmEng, a number of irregular verbs have become regularized, while remaining irregular in EngEng:

(a) In many instances, it is only the voicing of the past tense morpheme -*(e)d* which has been changed to regularize the verb:

	EngEng	NAmEng
Present	Past & Past Participle	Past & Past Participle
burn	burnt	burned
dwell	dwelt	dwelled
learn	learnt	learned
smell	smelt	smelled
spell	spelt	spelled
spill	spilt	spilled
spoil	spoilt	spoiled

(b) In some irregular EngEng verbs, there is a vowel change from /i/ in the present to /ɛ/ in the past and past participle forms. The NAmEng forms retain the present tense vowel in the following cases, as well as voicing the ending:

	EngEng	USEng
Present	Past & Past Participle	Past & Past Participle
dream	dreamt /drɛmt/	dreamed /drimd/
kneel	knelt	kneeled
lean	leant	leaned
leap	leapt	leaped

The NAmEng forms are also possible now in EngEng and the EngEng forms may still be found in formal language and poetry in NAmEng.

(c) In a few instances, the NAmEng forms are more irregular than the EngEng forms:

Present	*EngEng* Past & Past Participle	*NAmEng* Past	Past Participle
dive	dived	dove	dived
fit	fitted	fit	fitted
sneak	sneaked	snuck	snuck
get	got	got	gotten

NAmEng also uses *dived, fitted,* and *sneaked* for the past tense, but the irregular forms are more frequent:

> *He dove/dived in head first*
> *That suit fit/fitted me last week*
> *He snuck/sneaked around the corner*

The past participle *gotten* is not used in EngEng. In NAmEng it was formerly restricted to being used in the sense of 'obtain' or 'acquire':

> *I've gotten a new car since I last saw you*

Now, however, *gotten* can be used in all meanings except for 'have' in NAmEng, e.g.:

> *We have gotten home late again*
> *We've gotten together every June*
> *We had already gotten off the train when it was hit*
> *They've gotten me into trouble again*

but

> *I've got plenty to eat*
> *I've got the idea now* (= 'I understand')

2   Derivational

(a) One way of making or 'deriving' new verbs is to add a verb-forming suffix or prefix onto a noun or adjective: e.g. *symbol—symbolize, ripe—ripen, frost—defrost.* While it is usually the case that the same derivational suffixes are productive in both varieties of English, NAmEng tends perhaps to be more productive in its derivations, i.e. some affixes are used on classes of words or with particular senses of words where they would not be used in EngEng. While many such derived words are considered 'jargon' and not accepted into common use in NAmEng, those which are accepted are often borrowed quickly into EngEng.

　Two verb-forming affixes which are somewhat more productive in USEng than EngEng are:
  -ify as in *citify, humidify, uglify*
  -ize as in *burglarize, decimalize, hospitalize, rubberize, slenderize*

(b) Another way of forming new words is by simply changing a word's grammatical class, e.g. using a noun as a verb. This process is common to both varieties, with innovations spreading rapidly from one to the other. Again, there is more of a tendency to form new words in this way in USEng than in EngEng, e.g.:

Noun	Verb
an author	*to author*
a host	*to host ('We hosted a reunion last week')*
a sky-rocket	*to sky-rocket ('Prices are sky-rocketting this year')*
pressure	*to pressure* (EngEng *to pressurize*)
a room	*to room ('I room at that house')*

4.1.1.2   Auxiliaries

An auxiliary verb, as the name implies, does not exist as an independent verb in a sentence but must combine with a lexical verb to form a verb phrase. Different auxiliaries have various functions, such as entering into specific syntactic processes (question formation, negative contraction), expressing aspect (progressive and perfective), and expressing modality (volition, probability, obligation).

1   *Modal auxiliaries.* Several of the modals are used with a different frequency or meaning in NAmEng than in EngEng:

(a) *shall. Shall* is rarely used in NAmEng, except in legal documents or very formal styles, and is replaced by *will* (or *should* in questions with first person subjects). The negative form *shan't* is even rarer in USEng. Both varieties also often use the contracted form *'ll*.

EngEng	NAmEng & EngEng
I shall tell you later	*I will tell you later/I'll tell you later*
Shall I drink this now?	*Should I drink this now?*
I shan't be able to come	*I won't be able to come*

(b) *should.* As well as expressing obligation and tentativeness, *should* in EngEng can also have a hypothetical sense when it occurs in a main clause with a first person subject followed by a conditional clause. This use is mainly restricted to older speakers and writers. In NAmEng (and with younger EngEng speakers), *would* is used instead in such sentences:

(Older) EngEng: *I should enjoy living here if I could afford to do so*
NAmEng & younger EngEng: *I would enjoy living here if . . .*

(c) *would.* USEng has two uses for this modal that are much less usual in EngEng. First, *would* can be used in expressing a characteristic or habitual activity in USEng:

> *When I was young, I would go there every day*

In EngEng either the simple past or the verb with the modal *used to* would probably be used (this is also possible in USEng):

> *When I was young, I* $\left\{ \begin{array}{l} \textit{went} \\ \textit{used to go} \end{array} \right\}$ *there every day*

Second, while in EngEng *would* cannot be used to express a hypothetical state if this is already signalled by the verb or by a conditional clause, in many USEng dialects *would* can be used in this way in informal speech:

> USEng only: *I wish I would have done it*
> EngEng & USEng: *I wish I had done it*
>
> USEng only: *If I would have seen one, I would have bought it for you*
> EngEng & USEng: *If I had seen one, I would have bought it for you*

The second use of *would* is relatively recent in USEng and is more likely to be encountered in speech than in writing.

In EngEng, *would* and *will* are often used in a predictive sense, as in:

> *That will be the postman at the door*
> *That would be the building you want*
> *Would that be High Street over there?*

In USEng, it is more common to use the auxiliaries *should* or *must* in such sentences or not to have any auxiliary:

> *That* $\left\{ \begin{array}{l} \textit{is} \\ \textit{should be} \\ \textit{must be} \end{array} \right\}$ *the mailman at the door*
>
> *That* $\left\{ \begin{array}{l} \textit{is} \\ \textit{should be} \end{array} \right\}$ *the building you want*
>
> *Is that High Street over there?*

These other forms are also used in EngEng.

(d) *must*. The negative of epistemic *must* is *can't* in southern EngEng:

> *He must be in—his TV is on*
> *He can't be in—his car is gone*

(In the north-west of England, *mustn't* is used rather than *can't*).

In USEng, the most common negative of epistemic *must* is *must not*. Note that, unlike north-west EngEng, in USEng this cannot be contracted to *mustn't* without changing the meaning of the auxiliary to 'not be allowed':

> *He must not be in—his car is gone*   (epistemic)
> *You mustn't be in when we arrive*   ('not allowed')

However, *mustn't* can be epistemic in the past perfect:

> *He mustn't have been in*

Even in such cases, however, the uncontracted form is preferred in USEng.

(e) *use(d) to*. In questioning or negating sentences with the modal *used to*, EngEng can treat *used to* either as an auxiliary, in which case it inverts in questions and receives negation, or as a lexical verb requiring *do* for these constructions:

> *He used to go there*
> *Used he to go there?*   (auxiliary)
> *Did he use to go there?*   (lexical verb)
> *He used not to go there*   (auxiliary)
> *He didn't use to go there*   (lexical verb)

In USEng, *used to* is treated only as a lexical verb in these constructions, and this is also becoming increasingly the case in EngEng.

(f) *ought to*. USEng rarely uses this auxiliary in questions or negated forms. Instead, *should* is used:

EngEng	**USEng**
Ought we to eat that?	*Should we eat that?*
(older speakers)	

$You \left\{ \begin{array}{l} ought\ not \\ oughtn't \end{array} \right\}$ *to have said that*   *You shouldn't have said that*
You oughtn't have said that
(rare, formal)

Note that when *ought* is used in USEng in the negative, the *to* is usually deleted.

EngEng also can treat *ought to* as a lexical verb, similar to *used to*, in informal styles. These forms are considered non-standard in USEng:

> *Did you ought to eat that?*
> *You didn't ought to have said that*

(g) *dare* and *need*. Both of these auxiliaries are rare in USEng and usually occur in set phrases, such as:

Need I say more?
Persons under 18 need not apply
I dare say …

As with *used to*, USEng treats *dare* and *need* as lexical verbs in negating and questioning. EngEng also has this option:

{ EngEng (only): *Need you be so rude?* (auxiliary)
  USEng &
  EngEng: *Do you need to be so rude?* (verb)

{ EngEng (only): *You needn't be so rude!* (auxiliary)
  USEng &
  EngEng: *You don't need to be so rude!* (verb)

{ EngEng (only): *Dare I tell the truth?* (auxiliary)
  USEng &
  EngEng: *Do I dare (to) tell the truth?* (verb)

{ EngEng (only): *I daren't tell the truth* (auxiliary)
  USEng &
  EngEng: *I don't dare (to) tell the truth* (verb)

(h) *mayn't.* The contracted form of *may not* is only found in EngEng, and fairly rarely even there.

2 *do.* The auxiliary *do*, which is empty of meaning, is required in all varieties when constructing question and negative forms of simple verbs. (*Do you want this? I don't want this.*). It can also be used for polite commands or requests: *Do go on! Do sit down.* This last use is much less common in USEng, where *please* would be used instead.

3 *have, do have* and *have got.* A well-known grammatical difference between EngEng and USEng lies in the differing use of *have, do have* and *have got* to indicate possession. The situation has changed over the past few decades, so that what once were exclusively USEng or EngEng usages are no longer such.

Consider the following sentences:

(i)   *Have you any fresh cod?* (possess at present)
      I haven't any fresh cod
(ii) *Have you got (any) fresh cod?* (possess at present)
      I haven't got (any) fresh cod
(iii) *Do you have (any) fresh cod?* (possess at present)
      I don't have (any) fresh cod
(iv) *Do you have fresh cod?* (usually possess)
      I don't have fresh cod

In the (i) sentences, the lexical verb *have* functions as an auxiliary (i.e. it does not require the auxiliary *do* for question and negation; also, it can contract, as in *We've some fresh cod today*). Such sentences are usual, if somewhat formal or older, in EngEng, but are rare in USEng. Sentences like (ii) are usual in both varieties in more informal styles. Sentences of the (iii) type are the most usual ways of constructing question and negative forms indicating possession in USEng and are now also used in EngEng, although not long ago *do you have* could only be used in the habitual (iv) sense in EngEng. Sentences like those in (iv) are widely used in EngEng to express habitual possession but are not usual in USEng, where a paraphrase such as *Do you usually/ever have fresh cod* would be preferred. Thus an exchange like the following would make perfect sense to an EngEng speaker but might puzzle a USEng speaker:

Q   *Have you (got) any fresh cod?*
A   *No, I haven't*
Q   *Do you have fresh cod?*
A   *Yes, but we've already sold it all today*

In the past tense, the situation is more complicated.

(v)   *Had you any money at that time?*   (possessed)
       I hadn't any money at that time
(vi)   *Had you got any money at that*   (possessed, not
       time?*   acquired)
       I hadn't got any money at that time
(vii) *Did you have any money at that*   (habitually, or poss-
       time?*   essed at specific time)
       I didn't have any money at that time

The (v) sentences are used only by older EngEng speakers. The (vi) sentences are usual in EngEng but not usual in USEng. The (vii) sentences are widely used in both varieties.

Answers to the question types in (i) to (iii) above also differ between USEng and EngEng. In both varieties, the answer to a yes-no question can consist of just a subject and auxiliary(ies), the rest of the verb phrase being understood:

Did you go often?   Yes, I did
Have you seen them?   Yes, I have
Were you travelling a long time?   Yes, we were
Would they have done that?   Yes, they would (have)

However, for all of (i) to (iii), the EngEng reply would be *I have* or *I haven't* (even in (iii) where the auxiliary *do* is present), and the USEng reply would be *I do* or *I don't* (even in (i) and (ii) where the auxiliary is *have*) e.g.:

EngEng		*USEng*	
Q	*Do you have any fresh cod?*	Q	*Have you got fresh cod?*
A	*Yes, I have*	A	*Yes, I do*

4   In NAmEng, uninverted response questions of the type:

> *John went home*
> *He did?*

> *I'll do it*
> *You will?*

are very common, and indicate only mild surprise or interest. In EngEng inverted response questions such as:

> *John went home*
> *Did he?*

> *I'll do it*
> *Will you?*

are really the only possibility, though the NAmEng forms may be possible for some EngEng speakers as an indication of strong surprise.

4.1.1.3   Verb Phrase Substitutions with DO

In both EngEng and NAmEng, lexically empty *do* can substitute for a simple finite verb phrase which is the repetition of a verb phrase from the same or preceding sentence. *Do* is inflected for tense and person in such substitutions, e.g.:

> *John likes classical music and Mary does too* (= likes classical music)

> *John left work early today*
> *Oh? He did yesterday, too* (= left work early)

However, EngEng and NAmEng differ in the use of *do* substitution with an auxiliary. In EngEng *do* substitution can occur after most auxiliaries, *do* being inflected for tense (but not person). In NAmEng, *do* cannot be used in such instances. Instead of substitution, a deletion process is used whereby both the verb and its object are deleted. Also, if there are two aspectual auxiliaries, the second (in general) can be deleted. EngEng can also employ this deletion process. The following examples illustrate this:

Context	*Do-substitution* *(EngEng only)*	*Deletion* *(Both NAm & EngEng)*
Did he pass his exams?	*Yes, he did do*	*Yes, he did*
Have you cleaned your room?	*Yes, I have done*	*Yes, I have*
I haven't read this yet	*but I will do*	*but I will*

Will you have finished by next Monday?	Yes, I will have done	{ Yes, I will have { Yes, I will
I haven't bought one	but I may do	but I may
Will he come with us tonight?	He might do	He might
I haven't thrown them out	but I should do	but I should
Couldn't you do that later?	Yes, we could do	Yes, we could
Would you have recognized him?	No, I wouldn't have done	{ No, I wouldn't have { No, I wouldn't { (informal)

There are certain constructions even within finite verb phrases in which *do*-substitution cannot occur or are unusual in EngEng: when the passive voice is used; when the progressive aspect is used; and when 'semi-auxiliaries' (*happen to*, *be going to*, etc.) are used. (The acceptability of *do*-substitution with progressive aspect, semi-auxiliaries, and negated auxiliaries is also subject to regional variation in EngEng.) Where *do*-substitution is not acceptable, deletion occurs:

Context	Do-substitution (EngEng only)	Deletion (NAmEng and EngEng)
Passive Voice		
Were you fired?	*Yes, I was done	Yes, I was
Have you been injured?	*Yes, I have been done	{ Yes, I have been { Yes, I have
Progressive Aspect		
Are you working now?	?Yes, I am doing	Yes, I am
Will you be gardening tomorrow?	?Yes, we will be doing	{ Yes, we will be { Yes, we will
He must have been driving home	?Yes, he must have been doing	{ Yes, he must have been { Yes, he must have
Semi-auxiliary		
I haven't written to her yet	?but I'm going to do	but I'm going to
We didn't mean to fall in love	?We just happened to do	We just happened to
Negated Auxiliary		
I wanted to go	?but I couldn't do	but I couldn't
Have you read that yet?	No, I haven't done	No, I haven't
We stayed out late	but we shouldn't have done	but we shouldn't have

Some forms of AusNZEng and SAfEng are like NAmEng in not having *do*-substitution with auxiliaries. It is not common, either, in IrEng or ScotEng.

4.1.1.4 Verb Phrases

1 Certain verbs, like *give, show, tell, bring* take two objects, a direct object (DO) and an indirect object (IO). The indirect object, which is semantically a 'recipient', can occur with a preposition (usually *to* or *for*) after the DO, or it can occur before the DO without a preposition:

> John gave the book to Mary
>   DO   IO

> John gave Mary the book
>   IO   DO

When the DO is a pronoun, USEng requires the order DO + preposition + IO, as does southern EngEng:

> **USEng and Southern EngEng**
>
> John gave it to Mary
> *John gave Mary it

When both the DO and IO are pronouns, EngEng allows both orderings. It also permits deletion of the preposition in the first pattern, although this construction is somewhat old-fashioned except in northern EngEng:

USEng	*Southern EngEng*	*Northern EngEng*
John gave it to me	John gave it to me	John gave it to me
	John gave me it	John gave me it
		John gave it me

When comparing passive and active versions of a sentence, it can be seen that the DO of the active sentence corresponds to the subject (S) of the passive, and the S of the active corresponds to the object of a *by* prepositional phrase (OP) of the passive (or is deleted):

> Active: *John hit Mary*
>   S   DO
>
> Passive: *Mary was hit (by John)*
>   S   OP

In passive versions of double-object verbs like those above, there are usually two possible nouns which can be subjects—the DO or the IO of the active version:

> *The book was given to Mary by John*
> *Mary was given the book by John*

In USEng, when the active DO is used as the passive subject, the IO must occur with a preposition:

> *The book was given to Mary by John*
> **The book was given Mary by John*

Both sentences are allowed in EngEng. Also, in some varieties of USEng, when the DO is a pronoun, the IO cannot be used as a passive subject:

> **Mary was given it by John*

Again, however, this is possible in EngEng.

2   The verb *like* may take an infinitive (or infinitive clause) or an *-ing* participle (or clause) as its object:

Infinitive:	*I like to skate*	*I like to photograph animals in the wild*
-ing Participle:	*I like skating*	*I like photographing animals in the wild*

In EngEng the *-ing* participle construction is preferred.

When the object of *like* is a clause and the subject of that clause is not coreferential with the subject of *like*, then a *for . . . to* infinitive can be used in USEng. The normal *to* infinitive is usually used in such instances in EngEng.

EngEng & USEng	**USEng**
We'd like you to do this now	*We'd like for you to do this now*

3   In EngEng the copular verbs *seem, act, look* and *sound* can be followed directly by an indefinite noun phrase. In USEng, these verbs must be followed first by the preposition *like; seem* can also be followed by the infinitive *to be*:

EngEng	**USEng/EngEng**
It seemed a long time	*It seemed like a long time*
He seems an intelligent man	*He seems to be an intelligent man*
John acted a real fool	*John acted like a real fool*
That house looks a nice one	*That house looks like a nice one*
That sounds a bad idea	*That sounds like a bad idea*

4   *Come* and *go* may be followed by another verb either in a *to +* infinitive construction or conjoined by *and*:

We are coming to see you soon

He went $\left\{ \begin{array}{l} and\ fixed \\ to\ fix \end{array} \right\}$ it yesterday

When *come* and *go* are uninflected (both for tense and person), the *to* or *and* are often dropped in USEng, but not usually in EngEng:

EngEng/NAmEng	**USEng**
We'll come to see you soon	We'll come see you soon
Go and fix it now	Go fix it now
Can I come and have a cup of coffee with you?	Can I come have a cup of coffee with you?

NAmEng is also much more likely than EngEng to delete *to* after *help* when followed by another verb, even when *help* is inflected:

EngEng and NAmEng	**NAmEng**
I'll help to mow the lawn	I'll help mow the lawn
John helped us to mow the lawn	John helped us mow the lawn

5   When the verb *order* is followed by a passive verb, *to be* is often deleted in USEng, leaving the passive participle:

EngEng/USEng	**USEng**
He ordered the men to be evacuated	He ordered the men evacuated
We ordered that to be done immediately	We ordered that done immediately

6   The verb *want* can be followed directly by the adverbs *in* and *out* in USEng. In EngEng *want* must be followed first by an infinitive:

EngEng	**USEng**
I wanted $\left\{ \begin{array}{l} to\ come\ in \\ to\ be\ let\ in \end{array} \right\}$	I wanted in
The dog wants to go out	The dog wants out

Also, *want* can be used in the sense of 'need' in EngEng with an inanimate subject:

The house wants painting

This is not possible in NAmEng.

7   The verb *wonder* can be followed by a finite clause introduced by
if, *whether*, or a *wh*-relative pronoun in both varieties:

> *I wonder if/whether he is coming*
> *I wonder where he went*

In EngEng, *wonder* can also be followed by a clause introduced by
that (*that* is actually optional). In USEng, a periphrastic construction, or a different verb, is used instead:

EngEng:	*I wonder (that) he did any work at all!*
USEng:	*It's a wonder that he did any work at all!*

EngEng:	*I wonder (that) he is not here*
USEng:	*I'm surprised that he is not here*

8   The verb *decide* can be used as a causative verb in EngEng:

Non-causative:	*He decided to go because of that*
Causative:	*That decided him to go* (i.e., 'caused him to decide . . .')

In USEng, *decide* cannot be used as a causative; instead, a
periphrastic phrase must be used, such as:

> Periphrastic causative: *That made him decide to go*

9   There are a few verbs in EngEng and USEng which differ in the
prepositions or prepositional adverbs they collocate with:

EngEng	USEng
to battle with/against (the enemy)	*to battle*
to check up on	*to check out*
to fill in (a form)	*to fill out*
to meet (an official = have a meeting)	*to meet with*
to prevent (something becoming . . .)	*to prevent from*
to protest at/against/over (a decision)	*to protest*
to stop (someone doing . . .)	*to stop from*
to talk to	*to talk with/to*
to visit	*to visit with*

10   In EngEng, the negative form of the first person plural
imperative, *let's*, can be either *let's not* or, more informally, *don't let's*.
Only *let's not* is used in standard USEng.

11   In formal styles, the subjunctive is used more often in USEng
than in EngEng in *that*- clauses after verbs of ordering, asking, etc.

and in conditional clauses. Both varieties can replace the subjunctive in such sentences with *that...should* + infinitive or with *to* + infinitive especially in more informal styles:

USEng—formal	*EngEng & USEng—less formal*
We recommended that he be released	*We recommended that he should be released*
It is necessary that you do it	*It is necessary* $\begin{cases} \textit{that you should do it} \\ \textit{for you to do it} \end{cases}$
We ask that you inform us as soon as possible	*We ask you to inform us as soon as possible*
If this be the case, ...	*If this* $\begin{cases} \textit{should be the case,...} \\ \textit{is the case,...} \end{cases}$

12 Clauses representing hypothetical situations are often introduced by *if*, as in:

If I had been there, I could have fixed it
If you (should) need help, please call me
If this situation were to continue, the authorities would have to take action

In EngEng, hypothetical clauses can also be formed without using *if* by inverting the subject and verb or first auxiliary:

Had I been there, I could have fixed it
Should you need help, please call me
Were this situation to continue, the authorities would have to take action

Such constructions are considered very formal in USEng.
13 There is a strong tendency in NAmEng to use simple past tense forms for recently completed events where EngEng would use the present perfect, e.g.:

NAmEng: *So you finally arrived!*
EngEng: *So you've finally arrived!*

(See also 4.1.3(6), page 64, and ScotEng, IrEng.)

4.1.2 The Noun Phrase

There are few differences between EngEng and USEng as regards the noun phrase, and most are non-systematic in nature.

4.1.2.1 Morphology

1 As with verbal endings (4.1.1.1(2), page 45), certain noun endings are more productive in USEng than in EngEng, e.g.:

-cian:	*mortician* ('undertaker'); *beautician* ('hairdresser')
-ee:	*retiree, draftee, interviewee*
-ery:	*eatery, bootery, winery, hatchery*
-ster	*teamster, gamester*

In general, there is a greater tendency in USEng to use nominalizations than in EngEng.

2   For a few words, the derivational ending or the base word that the ending is put on to is different:

EngEng	**USEng**
candidature	*candidacy*
centenary	*centenial*
cookery (*book*)	*cook* (*book*)
racialist, racialism (adjective base)	*racist, racism* (noun base)
sparking plug	*spark plug*
stationers	*stationery shop*
transport (no ending)	*transportation*

3   Parallel to nouns being used as verbs (4.1.1.1(2), page 45), verbs can be used as nouns. Again this tends to occur more in USEng than in EngEng, especially with verb-preposition combinations:

Verb	**Noun**
to cook out(*-side*)	*a cook-out* ('an outdoor barbeque')
to know how (to do something)	*the know-how*
to run (someone) *around*	*the runaround*
to run down (e.g. a list)	*the rundown*
to be shut in	*a shut-in* ('an invalid')
to stop over (somewhere)	*a stop over*
to try (someone) *out*	*a try-out* ('an audition')

4.1.2.2   Noun Class

1   Collective nouns such as *team, faculty, family, government*, etc. often take plural verb agreement and plural pronoun substitution in EngEng but nearly always take singular agreement and singular pronoun substitution in USEng. While both singular and plural agreement and pronoun substitution with collective nouns are found in both varieties, the choice depends on whether the group referred to by the noun is seen as acting as individuals or as a single unit. There is a tendency in EngEng to stress the individuality of the members, which is reflected in plural verb agreement and pronoun substitution, whereas USEng strongly tends to stress the unitary function of the

group, which is reflected in singular verb and pronoun forms. Mixed agreement can also be found in USEng:

EngEng
Your team are doing well this year, aren't they?

USEng
Your team is doing well this year $\begin{cases} \textit{isn't it?} \\ \textit{aren't they?} \end{cases}$

2 *Count vs. mass nouns.* Count nouns have the following characteristics (among others): they normally occur with an article; they can occur with the indefinite article and cardinal numbers; and they have a plural. Mass nouns, on the other hand, have the opposite characteristics: they can occur with no article; they cannot occur with the indefinite article or cardinal numbers; and they are invariably singular. There are a few nouns which differ in count-mass class membership in the two varieties, e.g.:

(a) *lettuce* has characteristics of both a count and mass noun in EngEng, but it is only a mass noun in many varieties of USEng. It requires a partitive head noun to indicate quantity in USEng:

	EngEng	**USEng** (mass only)
Mass:	*I like lettuce*	*I like lettuce*
Count:	*a lettuce*	*a head of lettuce*
	two lettuces	*two heads of lettuce*

(b) *sport* is a count noun in both varieties but it can also be used as an abstract mass noun in EngEng:

	EngEng	**USEng** (count only)
Count:	*Football is a sport I like*	*Football is a sport I like*
	I like all team sports	*I like all team sports*
Mass:	*John is good at sport*	*John is good at sports*

(c) *accommodation/-s* is an abstract mass noun in both varieties, but instead of being invariably singular as is normal for mass nouns, it is invariably plural in USEng:

EngEng	**USEng**
Good accommodation is hard to find here	*Good accommodations are hard to find here*

3 *Zero plurals.* Some nouns retain the same form for singular and plural (they are said to have a 'zero plural' form), e.g. *sheep*. They

differ from invariably singular or plural nouns (like *bread, pants*) in that verb agreement does vary from singular to plural even though the noun form does not. There are a few nouns which differ in taking zero plurals in the two varieties, e.g.:

(a) *shrimp* can take a zero plural in USEng but must take a normal plural in EngEng:

EngEng	*USEng*
A shrimp fell on the floor	A shrimp fell on the floor
How many shrimps can you eat?	How many $\left\{\begin{array}{l}shrimp \\ shrimps\end{array}\right\}$ can you eat?

(b) *Inning* has the plural form *innings* in USEng. In EngEng, the singular form is *innings* and it has a zero plural:

EngEng	*USEng*
There is one innings left to play	There is one inning left to play
There are two innings in a cricket match	There are two innings in a cricket match

(c) When quantitative nouns such as *thousand, million*, etc. are used as modifiers and preceded by a cardinal number, they do not take plural inflection in either variety:

> *five thousand people*
> *three million dollars*

However, when the modified noun is deleted, in EngEng (especially in journalistic EngEng) the plural form of the quantitative noun can be used, while in USEng only the singular can be used:

EngEng only:	*The government have cut defence spending by three millions*
USEng (and EngEng):	*The government has cut defense spending by three million*

4.1.2.3   Articles

1   There are a number of count nouns in both varieties which do not require an article when used in an abstract-generic sense, usually with certain verbs or prepositions: e.g. *in spring, to go by car, to be at church*. However, there are a few such nouns which have this property in one variety but not the other:

EngEng	**USEng**
to be in hospital	*to be in the hospital*
$to \begin{Bmatrix} be\ at \\ go\ to \end{Bmatrix} university$	$to \begin{Bmatrix} be\ at \\ go\ to \end{Bmatrix} a\ university$
$to \begin{Bmatrix} be\ in \\ go\ to \end{Bmatrix} a\ class$	$to \begin{Bmatrix} be\ in \\ go\ to \end{Bmatrix} class$

2   When referring to events in the past, EngEng does not require the definite article before the phrase *next day*. This construction is more usual in written EngEng:

EngEng	**US & EngEng**
Next day, the rains began	*The next day, the rains began*
I saw him next day	*I saw him the next day*

3   EngEng does not use the definite article in the phrase *in future* in the meaning 'from now on', while USEng does:

EngEng: *In future, I'd like you to pay more attention to detail*
USEng: *In the future, I'd like you to pay more attention ...*
Both: *In the future, all homes will be heated by solar energy*

4   In temporal phrases beginning with *all*, the definite article can optionally appear before the noun in EngEng: *all afternoon* and *all the afternoon* are equally acceptable. In USEng, the construction without the article is by far the more frequent. If the sentence in which the phrase appears is negated, both varieties use the construction without the article: *I haven't seen him all year.*
5   In phrases beginning with *half* followed by some unit of measure, EngEng usually requires an indefinite article before the unit of measure. In USEng, the indefinite article can also come before *half*:

EngEng	**USEng**
half an hour	*a half hour* or *half an hour*
half a dozen (eggs)	*a half dozen* or *half a dozen*
half a pound (of carrots)	*a half pound* or *half a pound*

4.1.2.4   Order of Attributes

1   In the written standard, especially in newspapers, EngEng generally places personal attributes after the person named, whereas in USEng the attributes tend to precede the name, often without a definite article:

EngEng	*USEng*
John Smith, the lanky Californian teenage tennis star, won another major tournament today	*Lanky Californian teenage tennis star John Smith won another major tournament today.*
Margaret Thatcher, the British Prime Minister, arrived in Washington today	*British Prime Minister Margaret Thatcher arrived in Washington today*

2   For names of rivers, EngEng places the word *river* before the name of the river, while NAmEng uses the opposite order:

EngEng	*NAmEng*
the River Thames	*the Mississippi River*
the River Avon	*the Hudson River*

4.1.2.5   Pronouns

1   The indefinite pronoun *one* occurs in EngEng in formal and educated usage, both spoken and written, while in NAmEng it is usually found only in formal written style. *You* is used instead of *one* in informal styles of both varieties:

Formal: *One has to be careful about saying things like that*
Informal: *You have to be careful about saying things like that*

In EngEng when the indefinite pronoun *one* is used in a sentence, any coreferential pronoun in the sentence must also be *one* (or a form of it), while *he* or *she* (or forms of them) can be used in NAmEng:

EngEng and NAmEng (formal/educated)	*NAmEng*
If one tries hard enough, one will always succeed	*If one tries hard enough, he/she will always succeed*
One must be honest with oneself	*One must be honest with himself/herself*
One shouldn't be extravagant with one's money	*One shouldn't be extravagant with his/her money*

2   EngEng uses both reciprocal pronouns *each other* and *one another*, while USEng uses mainly *each other*, with *one another* (like *one*) being restricted to formal styles.
3   Possessive pronouns have two forms in both varieties: a modifier form and a nominal form:

Modifier:	*That is their car*
	This is my cat
Nominal:	*That car is theirs*
	This cat is mine

In EngEng, the nominal form can be used as a locative when referring to someone's living quarters, while in USEng the modifier form with noun is used in such cases:

EngEng:	*Can we come round to yours tonight?*
	We left his about an hour ago
USEng:	*Can we come around to your place tonight?*
	We left his house about an hour ago

4.1.3 Adjectives and Adverbs

1   In some varieties of USEng, a comparative adjective can be used in the phrase *all the ADJ* for emphasis or intensification: *Is that all the better you can do? This is all the bigger they grow.* EngEng does not employ this construction; instead, *any* is used with the comparative adjective (as it is also in USEng): *Can't you do any better (than that)? They don't grow any bigger (than this).*

2   The adjective *real* is sometimes used as an adverb in informal USEng as in *a real good meal.* EngEng and more formal USEng can only have the adverbial form *really* in such instances: *a really good meal.*

3   The comparative adjective *different* is usually followed by *from* (or sometimes *to*) in EngEng, while in USEng it is more usually followed by *than*:

EngEng:	*This one is different from the last one*
	This is different from what I had imagined
USEng:	*This one is different than the last one*
	This is different than what I had imagined

4   One particular adverbial ending is much more productive in USEng than in EngEng: *-wise.* While this ending is used to make nouns into manner adverbials in both varieties, it is also used in USEng to mean 'as far as X is concerned'; as in: *classwise, foodwise, timewise, weatherwise.* This usage is somewhat stigmatized.

5   Adverb placement is somewhat freer in USEng than in EngEng. Those adverbials which can occur medially, before the verb, are placed after the first auxiliary in EngEng if there is one: *They will* never *agree to it. You could* always *have called us first.* In USEng, such adverbs can occur either before or after the auxiliary: *They* never *will agree to it,* or *They will* never *agree to it. You* probably *could have done it yourself,* or *You could* probably *have done it yourself.*

6   The adverbs *yet* and *still* cannot occur with the simple past tense in EngEng, but they can do so in USEng. EngEng uses the present perfect in such cases.

EngEng and USEng (pres. perfect)	USEng only (simple past)
I haven't bought one yet	*I didn't buy one yet*
Have you read it already?	*Did you read it already?*

7   When the verb *to be* is used in the perfective with the meaning 'to go' or 'to come', the pronominal place adverbs *here* and *there* can be deleted in EngEng and CanEng, but not in USEng:

EngEng and CanEng: *Has the milkman been yet?*
Did you go to the market with them yesterday? No, I'd already been

USEng: *Has the milkman been here yet?*
Did you go to the market with them yesterday? No, I'd already been there

8   The ordinals *first(ly)*, *second(ly)*, etc. are used in both varieties as conjunctive adverbs in the listing of objects, actions, ideas, etc. While both varieties also use the enumerative adverbial phrase *first of all*, only USEng regularly uses *second of all*, *third of all*, etc. in such passages, although this would not be found in formal writing.

9   The adverb *momentarily* means 'for a moment' in both varieties. However, in USEng it can also mean 'in a moment':

Both: *He was momentarily stunned*   (for a moment)
US only: *I'll do it momentarily*   (in a moment)

Similarly, the adverb *presently* means 'soon' in both varieties, but in USEng can also mean 'at present' (when the verb is in the present tense):

Both: *They will be here presently*   (soon)
US only: *They are presently here*   (at present)

10   Adverbs ending in -*ward* in EngEng denote a purely directional motion while those ending in -*wards* can denote manner of movement also: *backward* ('movement to the back'), *backwards* ('movement back-first'). In USEng -*ward* no longer has a purely directional denotation for most speakers and such adverbs are used interchangeably, e.g.: *frontward(s)*. NAmEng has the forms *toward* and *towards* (identical in meaning). EngEng has only *towards*.

11   The time adverb *anymore* is used in both varieties in negative contexts, as in *I don't do that anymore* (= 'I no longer do that'). In some dialects of NAmEng (particularly Pennsylvania, upstate New

York, Ontario and the Mid-West), *anymore* can also be used in positive contexts with the meaning 'nowadays'. Implied in this usage is that whatever is being said to happen nowadays did not use to be the case: the sentence *He comes here a lot anymore* means that he comes here a lot nowadays and did not use to come here a lot. (For a possible origin of this feature, see 5.2.2, page 89.)

12 *Ever* can be used as an intensifier (without meaning 'at some time') in both varieties, but in different contexts. In EngEng it is cor̄monly used with the intensifier *so* before adjectives:

> EngEng: *She is ever so nice*
> *That match was ever so close*

In NAmEng, *ever* can be used informally to intensify verbs in exclamations which have subject-verb inversion:

> NAmEng: *Did he ever hit the ball hard!*
> *Has she ever grown!*
> *Am I ever tired!*

13 In CanEng, the adverbial phrase *as well* can occur sentence-initially, whereas in EngEng and USEng it usually appear; after the item it modifies:

> CanEng: *This has always applied to men. As well,*
> *it now applies to women*

> EngEng and USEng: *This has always applied to men. It now applies to women as well*

4.1.4 Prepositions

1 There are a few prepositions which differ in form in the two varieties:

EngEng USEng

behind *in back of* as in *I put it* $\left\{\begin{array}{l}\textit{behind}\\\textit{in back of}\end{array}\right\}$ *the shed*

out of *out* as in *He threw it* $\left\{\begin{array}{l}\textit{out of}\\\textit{out}\end{array}\right\}$ *the window*

round *around* as in *She lives just* $\left\{\begin{array}{l}\textit{round}\\\textit{around}\end{array}\right\}$ *the corner*

2 Some prepositions which are used identically in most contexts in both EngEng and USEng differ in usage in certain contexts. The majority of such cases occur in expressions of time.

(a) Difference in preposition used:

(i) in phrases indicating duration of time, EngEng uses *for* where NAmEng has a choice of *for* or *in*:

	EngEng & NAmEng	NAmEng only
I haven't seen him:	*for weeks*	*in weeks*
	for ages	*in ages*

(ii) EngEng speakers use the preposition *at*, meaning 'time when', with holiday seasons, as in *at the weekend, at Christmas* (the season, not the day). USEng speakers generally use *over* in such cases: *over the weekend, over Christmas*. EngEng also permits *over* in these cases, and NAmEng also has *on the weekend*.

(iii) in USEng the preposition *through* can mean 'up to and including', as in *Monday through Friday, September 1 through October 15*. In EngEng the 'inclusiveness' must be stated separately if ambiguity is possible: e.g. *Monday to Friday* (*inclusive*) or *Monday up to and including Friday*.

(iv) In expressing clock-time, EngEng uses the prepositions *to* and *past* the hour while USEng also can use *of*, *till* and *after* (this differs regionally in the USA):

EngEng and USEng	USEng only
twenty to three	*twenty of three* or *twenty till three*
five past eight	*five after eight*

(v) *In* and *on* have some differences in non-temporal contexts:

EngEng	USEng
to be in a team	*to be on a team*
to live in a street	*to live on a street*
to be in a sale	*to be on sale*

(N.B. *on sale* in EngEng simply means *for sale*.)

(b) Difference in presence of a preposition:

(i) The preposition (usually *on*) is often omitted in USEng before a specific date or day of the week that indicates a time removed from the present:

EngEng	USEng
The sale started on Jan. 1st	*The sale started Jan. 1*
(said: 'on January the first')	(said: 'January first')
I'll do it on Sunday	*I'll do it Sunday*

(ii) The preposition can be deleted in USEng before temporal nouns indicating repetition or habitual action (the nouns must become plural if deletion occurs):

EngEng and USEng	*USEng*
He works by day and studies at night	He works days and studies nights.
On Saturdays we go to London	Saturdays we go to London.

(iii) In EngEng temporal prepositional phrases, inversion of the noun and the words *this, that, next* or *last* can occur in formal styles: *on Sunday next, during January last*. Such inversion does not occur in USEng, and the preposition is deleted in the uninverted forms (as in (i) above): *next Sunday, last January*.

(iv) In phrases denoting a period of time from or after a given time, the preposition *from* is often deleted in EngEng, but cannot be deleted in USEng:

EngEng	*USEng*
a week this Tuesday	a week from this Tuesday

EngEng also allows inversion in such phrases with no preposition: *Saturday fortnight, Tuesday week*. This does not occur in USEng.

(v) In EngEng, there is a difference in meaning between the phrases *to be home* and *to be at home*:

| Is John at home? | (Is he physically there?) |
| Is John home? | (Has he arrived there?) |

USEng can use the second phrase (without the preposition) in the meaning of the first.

(vi) In EngEng, the preposition *from* can be deleted after the verbs *excused* and *dismissed*:

He was excused games at school
He was dismissed the service

This is not possible in USEng.

3 In sentences such as *The cake has flowers on it, The box with toys in it is mine*, where an inanimate concrete object is designated as having (or not having) a concrete object *in, on, round* or *off* it, the coreferential pronoun *it* can be deleted from the prepositional phrase in EngEng, but not in USEng:

EngEng	USEng
The soup has carrots in	*The soup has carrots in it*
I want some paper with lines on	*I want some paper with lines on it*
This shirt has two buttons off	*This shirt has two buttons off it*
What kind is that tree with flowers round?	*What kind is that tree with flowers around it?*
I'd like toast without butter on	*I'd like toast without butter on it*

4.1.5   Subordinators

1   The complex subordinators *as ... as* and *so ... as* are used with different frequencies in the two varieties. *So ... as* is fairly infrequent in USEng, being used mainly at the beginning of a clause, while in EngEng it tends to be used more than *as ... as*:

EngEng	USEng
It's not so far as I thought it was	*It's not as far as I thought it was*
So long as you're happy, we'll stay	*As long as you're happy, we'll stay*
Now we don't go there so much (as we used to)	*Now we don't go there as much (as we used to)*
That one isn't so nice (as the other)	*That one isn't as nice (as the other)*

In cases where *as ... as* is preferred in EngEng and used at the beginning of a clause, the first *as* may be dropped:

EngEng	USEng
Strange as it may seem, ...	*As strange as it may seem, ...*
Much as I would like to go, ...	*As much as I would like to go, ...*

2   In EngEng, the adverbs *immediately* and *directly* can function as subordinators. In USEng, they must modify a subordinator, such as *after*:

EngEng	USEng
Immediately we went, it began to rain	*Immediately after we went, it began to rain*
Go to his office directly you arrive	*Go to his office directly after you arrive*

4.2　Spelling and Punctuation Differences

4.2.1　Standard Spellings

There are several sets of regular spelling differences that exist between the English and American varieties of English. Some are due to American innovations or to overt attempts at spelling regularization (especially by Noah Webster in his 1806 dictionary). Others simply reflect the fact that English spelling was variable in earlier times and the two varieties chose different variants as their standard. Below is a list exemplifying the major spelling differences. No attempt has been made to include every word falling under the particular spelling correspondence; we have indicated if the set is a restricted one. CanEng usage in some cases follow USEng, in others EngEng, and in yet others is variable

	EngEng:	*USEng:*	
1	*-our*	*-or*	(but not in words
	colour	color	ending in *-or* signifying
	favour	favor	persons, e.g. *emperor*,
	honour	honor	*governor* in both varieties)
	labour	labor	
	odour	odor	
	vapour	vapor	
2	*-ou-*	*-o-*	(restricted lexical
	mould	mold	set; cf. *boulder* in
	moult	molt	both varieties)
	smoulder	smolder	
3	*-ae/oe-*	*-e-*	(in Greek borrowings;
	anaesthetic	anesthetic	USEng sometimes uses
	encyclopaedia	encyclopedia	EngEng spelling in
	mediæval	medieval	scholarly works)
	amoeba	ameba	
	foetus	fetus	
	manoeuvre	maneuver	
4	*en-*	*in-*	(restricted; cf. *envelope*,
	encase	incase	*incur* in both varieties;
	enclose	inclose	*inquire* also used in
	endorse	indorse	EngEng; EngEng spelling
	enquire	inquire	preferred in USEng in all
	ensure	insure	but last three items)
	enure	inure	
5	*-dgement*	*-dgment*	(EngEng spelling also
	abridgement	abridgment	possible in USEng)
	acknowledgement	acknowledgment	
	judgement	judgment	

6   **EngEng: -re**   **USEng: -er**
centre   center
fibre   fiber
litre   liter
metre   meter
spectre   specter
theatre   theater

7   **EngEng: -ce**   **USEng: -se**
defence   defense
licence (n.)   license (n. and v.)
offence   offense
practice (n.)   practise or practice
                    (n.)
pretence   pretense

8   **EngEng: -ise**   **USEng: -ize**   (USEng spelling is also
apologise   apologize   possible in EngEng;
capitalise   capitalize   CanEng spelling usually
dramatise   dramatize   has *-ize* when the
glamourise   glamorize   stem is transparent—
naturalise   naturalize   *capitalize, glamourize,*
satirise   satirize   *naturalize*—and *-ise*
                                        when it is not—*apologise,*
                                        realise; EngEng and
                                        NAmEng both normally
                                        have *advertise*)

9   **EngEng: -xion**   **USEng: -ction**   (USEng spelling also
connexion   connection   possible in EngEng;
deflexion   deflection   restricted, cf.
inflexion   inflection   *inspection* and *complexion*
retroflexion   retroflection   in both varieties)

10 **EngEng: doubled** **USEng: single**   (only before an ending
    consonant   **consonant**   that starts with a
counsellor   counselor   vowel, stress not on
kidnapper   kidnaper   last syllable of stem;
levelled   leveled   EngEng spelling also used
libellous   libelous   in USEng)
quarrelling   quarreling
travelled   traveled
worshipping   worshiping

11 **EngEng: single -l-** **USEng: double -l-** (before an ending that
fulfilment   fulfillment   starts with a consonant
instalment   installment   or at the end of a

skilful	*skillful*	polysyllabic word that
enthral	*enthrall*	has stress on the last
instil	*instill*	syllable)
fulfil	*fulfill*	

12 **EngEng: -gg-** **USEng: -g-** (restricted to a few
faggot ('bundle of *fagot* (but *faggot* words)
sticks) slang, 'homosexual')
waggon *wagon*

13 **EngEng: -st** **USEng: no ending** (restricted to a few
amidst *amid* words; USEng spelling
amongst *among* also possible in EngEng;
whilst *while* spelling differences
reflected in pronunciation)

14 **Miscellaneous**

EngEng	**USEng**	
buses	*busses* or *buses*	
cheque (banking)	*check*	
draught	*draft*	
gaol	*jail*	
gauge	*gage* or *gauge*	
jewellery	*jewelry*	
kerb	*curb*	
moustache	*mustache*	
plough	*plow*	
programme	*program*	
pyjamas	*pajamas* or *pyjamas*	
sorbet	*sherbet*	(different pronunciation)
speciality	*specialty*	(different pronunciation)
storey (of a building)	*story*	
sulphur	*sulfur*	
toffee	*taffy*	(different pronunciation)
tsar	*czar*	
tyre	*tire*	
whisky	*whiskey*	
woollen	*woolen*	

15 **EngEng:** **USEng: fused or** (in compounds and words
hyphenated **two separate** with stressed prefixes;
words **words** hyphen is usually kept
ash-tray *ashtray* (also in USEng if identical
EngEng) vowels are brought
book-keeper *bookkeeper* together or if stem be-
day-dream *daydream* gins with capital letter e.g.
dry-dock *dry dock* *anti-British, pre-eminent*)

flower-pot	*flower pot*
note-paper	*note paper*
anti-aircraft	*antiaircraft*
co-operate	*cooperate*
neo-classical	*neoclassical*
pre-ignition	*preignition*
pseudo-intellectual	*pseudointellectual*
ultra-modern	*ultramodern*

16 **EngEng: retains**   **USEng: diacritics**
    French diacritics   **not necessary**

café	*cafe*
élite	*elite*
entrée	*entree*
fête	*fete*
fiancée	*fiancee*
matinée	*matinee*

4.2.2 'Sensational' Spellings

In the USA many sensational (and non-standard) spellings which usually involve simplification of the spelling to reflect more closely the pronunciation are used to attract attention, especially in advertising and in tabloid newspapers; they may also be used on roadsigns to save space. The list below gives a sample of common nouns often spelled in a non-standard way; a list of proper nouns (brand names especially) would be exceedingly long.

Sensational	**Standard**
bi	*buy*
donut	*doughnut*
hi	*high*
kool	*cool*
kwik	*quick*
lo	*low*
nite, tonite	*night, tonight*
pleez	*please*
rite	*right*
sox	*socks*
thanx	*thanks*
tho	*though*
thru, thruway	*through, throughway*
U	*you*
Xing	*crossing*

4.2.3 Punctuation

There are very few punctuation differences between 'American' and 'English' types of English, and printers and publishers vary in their preference even within the two areas. Typically, however, British usage favours having a lower case letter for the first word of a sentence following a colon, as in:

> *There is only one problem: the government does not spend sufficient money on education*

whereas American usage more often favours a capital letter:

> *There is only one problem: The government does not spend sufficient money on education*

Also, normal British usage is to have a full-stop after a closing quotation mark, as in:

> *We are often told that 'there is not enough money to go round'.*

while American usage has the full-stop (AmEng *period*) before the closing quotation marks:

> *We are often told that 'there is not enough money to go round.'*

Note, however, that if a whole sentence is devoted to a quotation, usage agrees in having the full-stop before the quotation marks:

> *'There is not enough money to go round.'*

4.3 Vocabulary Differences

Perhaps the most noticeable differences between EngEng and NAmEng involve vocabulary. There are thousands of words which either differ in total meaning, or in one particular sense or usage, or are totally unknown in the other variety. (There are also a large number of idioms and colloquialisms which differ in the two varieties, but these will not be discussed here.)

Vocabulary differences between the two varieties are due to several factors. The most obvious is that new objects and experiences were encountered in North America which needed naming, either by adapting EngEng vocabulary or by creating new words: e.g., *corn* is the general English term for grain and denotes the most common grain crop, which is wheat in England but maize in North America; the word *robin* denotes a small, red-breasted warbler in England but a large, red-breasted thrush in North America; the words *panhandle* (the narrow part of a state extending outward like a pan's handle) and *butte* (an abrupt isolated hill with a flat top) denote features not found in Britain.

Technological and cultural developments which have occurred since the divergence of two varieties have also been a cause of differences in vocabulary: e.g. terms for parts of cars: US—*windshield*, Eng—*windscreen*; US—*trunk*, Eng—*boot*; terminology from different sports: US—(from baseball) *home run, bunt, pitcher*; Eng—(from cricket) *pitch, wicket, bowler*, etc.; differences in institutions of education: US—*high school* (14–18 year olds), *major* (= *main subject*), *co-ed* (female student); Eng—*public school* (= *private school*), *form* (educational level), *reader* (= *associate professor*), etc.

A third reason for vocabulary differences is the influence of other languages. USEng has borrowed many words (some of which have found their way into EngEng) from a variety of languages, including: American Indian languages—*hickory* (type of tree related to walnut), *hooch* (alcoholic liquor), *moccasin, muskie* (type of freshwater fish), *squash, toboggan*, and many words for indigenous flora, fauna and geographical features; Spanish—*mesa* (plateau), *tornado* (whirlwind), *tortilla* (thin flat maize bread); African languages—*goober* (peanut), *jazz, banjo*; and Yiddish—*schmaltz* (excessive sentimentality), *schlep* (to drag, carry), *schlock* (rubbish).

Finally, independent linguistic change within each variety may be the cause of some differences. One variety may preserve archaisms which the other has lost, or may introduce new meanings for old words which the other has not introduced. CanEng examples of archaisms include *chesterfield* (sofa, couch) and *reeve* (mayor, chief local government officer).

Words used in one variety are often borrowed into the other (unless the thing denoted does not occur in that area). The highest proportion of borrowings is from USEng to EngEng, although examples can be given for borrowings in both directions:

EngEng borrowings from USEng	*USEng borrowings from EngEng*
billion (a thousand million)	*copper* (*cop*)
brief-case	*penny*
cafeteria	*smog*
teenager	
radio	
snowplow (*snowplough*)	

In other cases, the differing word might not actually have been borrowed, but it has become known and understood in the other variety: e.g., most EngEng speakers know or will understand that *drapes* are curtains; and most USEng speakers know that a *flat* is an apartment. In still other cases, particularly with slang or idioms, a particular word or sense is not known at all by speakers of the other variety.

We can divide vocabulary differences into four major categories, although there is some overlap.

1 *Same word, different meaning.* This is the category of words which is potentially the most problematic for both foreign and native speakers of one variety, but such examples are few in number. They include:

Word	*EngEng meaning*	*USEng meaning*
homely	down to earth, domestic (= US *homey*)	ugly (of people)
nervy	nervous	bold, full of nerve, cheeky
pants	underpants	trousers
pavement	footpath, sidewalk	road surface
to tick off	to scold	to make angry

2 *Same word, additional meaning in one variety.* There are quite a few words of this type, some of which can cause communication problems between speakers of the two varieties. Often the additional meaning is due to a metaphorical extension of the common meaning:

Additional meaning in USEng

Word	*Meaning in common*	*Additional meaning in USEng*
bathroom	room with bath or shower and sink	room with toilet only
cute	endearing (e.g. of kittens)	attractive, charming (e.g. of adult people)
dumb	mute	stupid
good	fine, nice, etc.	valid (as of tickets, special offers)
regular	consistent, habitual	average (as in size), normal
school	institution of education at elementary level	all institutions of education, including universities
to ship	to transport by ship	to transport by ship, train, plane or truck

Additional meaning in EngEng

Word	Meaning in common	Additional meaning in EngEng
frontier	a wild, open space	border between two countries
leader	one who commands, guides, directs, is in front	an editorial
to mind	to heed, obey	to look after (as in *mind your head, mind the children*)
rug	a thick (usually wool) carpet	a thick (usually wool) wrap or coverlette (USEng *afghan*)
smart	intelligent	well-groomed
surgery	a medical operation or operating room	an office of any doctor

3   *Same word, difference in style, connotation, frequency of use.* While words differing in style, connotation or frequency will usually be understood by speakers of the other variety, it is the use of these types of words which often reveals which variety of English a person has learned. The example words below are marked for differences in style (formal vs. informal), connotation (positive vs. negative), or frequency (common vs. uncommon):

Word	EngEng usage	USEng usage
autumn	common; all styles	uncommon; poetic or formal (*fall* used instead)
clever ('smart, dexterous')	common; positive	less common; usually negative (i.e. 'sly')
to fancy ('to like, want')	common; informal	uncommon
fortnight	common; all styles	uncommon (archaic); poetic
perhaps	all styles	somewhat formal (*maybe* used instead)
quite (as in *quite good*)	negative or neutral	positive
row (/rɑu/; 'quarrel, disturbance')	common	uncommon

4   *Same concept or item, different word.* The majority of lexical differences between the two varieties are of this type. There are two sub-types within this category; that in which the corresponding word is not widely known in the other variety, and that in which the

corresponding word is known. Examples of the first type include:

USEng only	*Corresponds to EngEng*
emcee	*compère*
faucet	*tap*
muffler (on car)	*silencer*
rookie	*first year member* (e.g. on a team)
sophomore	*second year student*
washcloth	*face flannel*

EngEng only	*Corresponds to USEng*
dynamo	*generator*
hire purchase	*installment buying*
nought	*zero*
queue	*line*
spanner	*monkey wrench*
treacle	*molasses*

Examples of the second type include:

USEng	*EngEng*
to call (by telephone)	to ring
can	*tin*
to check ('to make a check mark')	to tick
couch, davenport	*sofa*
game (sports)	*match*
gas	*petrol*
to make a reservation	to book
sidewalk	*(paved streetside) path*

Finally, by way of further illustration, we give a brief and arbitrary selection of words that differ in particular semantic spheres. Note that some words, while identical in one semantic sphere or part of speech, can be different in another: e.g. both varieties use the words *hood* and *bonnet* to refer to two distinct types of head covering, but when referring to the covering of a car engine, USEng uses *hood* and EngEng uses *bonnet*. Likewise, while both varieties have the verb *to flex* with identical meaning, the noun *a flex* is used only in EngEng (and is unknown in USEng) to refer to an electric cord.

Food and Cooking

USEng	*EngEng*
cookie (plain)	*biscuit* (sweet)
biscuit	*scone*
cracker	*biscuit* (savory)

dessert	pudding
pudding	custard
custard	egg custard
jello	jelly
jelly	jam
crepe	pancake
hamburger meat	mince
roast (noun)	joint
eggplant	aubergine
zucchini	courgette
to broil	to grill
stove	cooker
bowl (e.g. for pudding)	basin
pitcher	jug

Clothing and Accessories

USEng	EngEng
garter	suspender
suspenders	braces
underpants (women's)	knickers
knickers	knickerbockers
smock	overall
overalls	dungarees
sweater (pullover)	jumper
jumper	dress worn over blouse
undershirt	vest
vest	waistcoat
pantyhose	tights
tuxedo	dinner jacket
barette	hairslide
changepurse	purse
purse	handbag
diaper	nappy

Household

USEng	EngEng
living room	sitting room
yard	garden
garden	vegetable or flower garden

buffet	*sideboard*
flashlight	*torch*
floorlamp	*standard lamp*
garbage can	*dustbin*
outlet/socket	*power point*
sheers	*net curtains*

Commerce

USEng	EngEng
mortician	*undertaker*
realtor	*estate agent*
travelling salesman	*commercial traveller*
drug store/ pharmacy	*chemist's shop*
hardware store	*ironmongers*
liquor store	*off-license store*
trade (noun)	*custom*

Transportation

USEng	EngEng
baby buggy	*pram (perambulator)*
station wagon	*estate car*
trailer/camper/ mobile home	*caravan*
pullman car (railway)	*sleeping car*
flatcar (railway)	*truck*
truck	*lorry*
pedestrian underpass	*subway*
subway	*underground railway*

5
Scottish and Irish English

5.1 Scottish English

English has been spoken in the south-east of Scotland for as long as it has been spoken in England. In the south-west of Scotland it dates from the middle ages. In the Highlands and Islands of northern and western Scotland, English has been spoken for only 200 years or so, and indeed Gaelic is still the native language of several tens of thousands of speakers from these areas.

A standardized form of language based on southern Scottish varieties and known as Scots was used at the Scottish court and in literature until the Reformation. Since that time, however, Scots has gradually been replaced in educated usage by Standard English, except in the literature of the likes of Burns and a number of more modern writers (there is currently a strong movement for the revival of Scots). The result is that today educated Scottish people speak and write a form of Standard English which is grammatically and lexically not very different from that used elsewhere, although they speak it with a very obviously Scottish accent. However, the non-standard dialects of southern and eastern Scotland, especially in rural areas, still resemble Scots in many respects and are radically different from most other varieties used in the English-speaking world. In the Highlands, where English was initially learned only in school, forms close to Scottish Standard English are used by all speakers. In this book we concentrate on Scottish Standard English as used and spoken by educated, middle-class urban Scots.

5.1.1 ScotEng Pronunciation: Vowels

ScotEng pronunciation is very different from that of most other varieties and may be difficult to understand for students who have learned EngEng or NAmEng. Table 5.1 and the recording illustrate a typical ScotEng vowel system:

Table 5.1   ScotEng Vowels*

/i/	bee, peer
/e/	bay, pair
/ɛ/	bed, merry, fern
/ɪ/	bid, bird, butt<u>er</u>, want<u>ed</u>
/ʌ/	putt, hurry, fur, sof<u>a</u>
/a/	bad, marry, bard, path, father, calm
/u/	put, boot, poor
/o/	boat
/ɔ/	pot, long, cough, fork, paw
/ai/	buy
/au/	bout
/ɔi/	boy

* *The words in table 5.1 are also used in the recording for NIrEng (see page 121).*

It will be observed at once that there are fewer vowels in this system than in any of the other varieties we have examined. This is due to the following factors:

1   ScotEng is rhotic. Therefore, the RP vowels /ɪə/, /ɛə/, /ʊə/ and /ɜ:/ (which arose in RP as a result of the loss of non-prevocalic /r/) do not occur in ScotEng, and words such as *sawed* and *soared* are distinct. Furthermore, it is a particular characteristic of ScotEng that even short vowels remain distinct before /r/. As a consequence of this, the following pairs are distinguished only by the presence or absence of /r/:

bee	/bi/	beer	/bir/
bay	/be/	bear	/ber/
fen	/fɛn/	fern	/fɛrn/
bid	/bɪd/	bird	/bɪrd/
hut	/hʌt/	hurt	/hʌrt/
bad	/bad/	bard	/bard/
moo	/mu/	moor	/mur/
row	/ro/	roar	/ror/
pot	/pɔt/	port	/pɔrt/

Note that *fern*, *bird*, *hurt* all have *different* vowels; however, they are often merged in middle-class speech.

2   The RP distinction between /æ/ and /ɑ:/ does not exist in most ScotEng varieties. We write /a/ for the vowel of *bad*, *bard*, *calm* etc. Note that *Pam* and *palm* are therefore homonyms—/pam/. However, some middle-class speakers do have this distinction, probably as a result of the influence of RP.

3   The RP distinction between /ʊ/ and /u:/ does not exist in most types of ScotEng. *Pool* and *pull* are homonyms—/pul/.

4   There is no RP-type distinction between /ɒ/ and /ɔ:/. We write /ɔ/ for both *cot* and *caught*. (*Fort* etc., of course, have /r/.)
5   Phonetically, the ScotEng vowels are monophthongs (with the exceptions of /ai/ = [ɛɪ] ~ [ɐɪ]; /au/ = [ɜʉ]; and /ɔi/). Both /ɪ/ = [ɪ⊢ ~ ə̣] and /ʌ/ are central vowels, and /u/ = [ʉ]. Length is not distinctive as it is in RP.

Interestingly, however, there is a distinction of length in ScotEng between the vowels of

    tide   *tied*
    booze *boos*
    greed *agreed*

with the items with inflectional endings (*-d*, *-s*) having longer vowels. Vowels are longer in final stressed open syllables than elsewhere, and this feature is preserved even where an inflection is added.
6   In words such as *serenity*, *obscenity*, the second syllable is often pronounced with /i/, as it is in *serene*, *obscene*, rather than with /ɛ/ as in RP.

5.1.2   ScotEng Pronunciation: Consonants

1   ScotEng consistently and naturally preserves a distinction between /ʍ/ and /w/: *which* /ʍɪč/, *witch* /wɪč/.
2   Initial /p/, /t/, /k/ are often unaspirated in ScotEng.
3   The consonant /r/ is most usually a flap [ɾ], as in *fern* [fɛɾn] (cf. RP [fɜ:n], USEng [fəɹn]). Some middle-class speakers, however, use the frictionless continuant [ɹ]. These are usually the same speakers who have merged /ɪ/, /ɜ/, /ʌ/ before /r/ (see above); thus they have *fern* as [fəɹn].
4   The glottal stop [ʔ] is a frequent realization of non-initial /t/.
5   /l/ may be dark in all positions; e.g. *lilt* [ɫəɫt].
6   The velar fricative /x/ occurs in a number of specifically ScotEng words. After front vowels it is usually realized as [ç]: e.g., *loch* [lɔx] 'lake'; *dreich* [drɪç] 'dull'. In Scots dialects /x/ occurs in many other words e.g. *nicht* = *night*: Scots dialect [nəçt], ScotEng [nɛɪt].

5.1.3   Non-systematic Differences between ScotEng and EngEng Pronunciation

A few words have distinctively Scottish, or at least non-RP, pronunciations in Scotland:

	ScotEng	**RP**
length	/lɛnθ/	/lɛŋθ/
raspberry	/rasbɛrɪ/	/rɑːzbrɪ/
realise	/rɪʌláiz/	/ríəlaiz/
though	/θo/	/ðou/
tortoise	/tɔrtɔiz/	/tɔːtəs/
with	/wɪθ/	/wɪð/

5.1.4   ScotEng Grammar

Most of the grammatical differences between ScotEng and EngEng are found at the level of informal speech. They include the following:

1   The full verb *have* behaves more like an auxiliary in ScotEng than in EngEng (see 4.1.1.2(3), page 49), i.e. in both the present and past tense it can contract and does not require *do*-support for yes-no questions or negation, e.g.:

> ScotEng: *He'd a good time last night*
> EngEng: *He had a good time last night*

> ScotEng: *Had you a good time last night?*
> EngEng: *Did you have a good time last night?*

2   As in NAmEng, *will* has replaced *shall* in most contexts. ScotEng goes further than NAmEng in having *will* with first person subjects in questions:

> ScotEng: *Will I put out the light?*
> others: *Shall/Should I put out the light?*

3   There is a tendency not to contract the negative element *not* in ScotEng, especially in yes-no questions. If an auxiliary is present in a negated sentence, the auxiliary usually contracts.

ScotEng	**EngEng**
Is he not going?	*Isn't he going?*
Did you not see it?	*Didn't you see it?*
He'll not go	*He won't go*
You've not seen it	*You haven't seen it*

4   In sentences like the following, *need* is a full verb with a verbal complement, as in USEng, rather than a modal, as in EngEng (see 4.1.1.2(1g), page 48):

> ScotEng: *I don't need to do that*
> EngEng: *I needn't do that*

Need can occur with a passive participle as its object, as it can in some regional US dialects, whereas most other varieties of English require the passive infinitive or present participle:

> ScotEng: *My hair needs washed*
> EngEng: *My hair needs washing*
> *My hair needs to be washed*

5 *Want* and *need* can have a directional adverb as object as in USEng (see 4.1.1.4(6), page 55):

> *He wants/needs out*

6 Certain stative verbs, especially *want* and *need*, can be used in the progressive aspect in ScotEng:

> *I'm needing a cup of tea*

7 As in USEng, *yet* can occur in ScotEng with non-perfective forms of the verb, while in EngEng it can only occur with the perfective (see 4.1.3(6), page 64):

> ScotEng: *Did you buy one yet?*
> EngEng: *Have you bought one yet?*
>
> ScotEng: *He is here yet*
> EngEng: *He is still here*

8 In EngEng the adverbial particle in compound verbs tends to come after the direct object, while in ScotEng it remains directly after the verb, as in many varieties of NAmEng:

ScotEng	**EngEng**
He turned out the light	*He turned the light out*
They took off their coats	*They took their coats off*

All of the above grammatical features are also found in NIrEng.

5.1.5 ScotEng Vocabulary and Idioms

The vocabulary of Scots and non-standard Scottish dialects differs very considerably from that of Standard English, to the extent that dictionaries or glossaries may be necessary for reading literature in Scots (e.g. Burns, McDiarmid). ScotEng, on the other hand, differs much less in its vocabulary from other varieties of English. The differences, nevertheless, are numerous enough. We give a brief list and discussion here of a few of the ScotEng lexical items which may be encountered.

	ScotEng	EngEng
1	*ashet*	*serving dish*
2	*aye*	*yes*
3	*brae*	*incline, hill*
4	*bramble*	*blackberry*
5	*burn*	*stream*
6	*carry-out*	*take-away*
7	*dram*	*drink*
8	*dreich*	*dull*
9	*folk*	*people*
10	*haar*	*sea mist*
11	*infirmary*	*hospital*
12	*to jag*	*to prick, jab*
13	*janitor*	*caretaker*
14	*loch*	*lake*
15	*to mind*	*to remember*
16	*outwith*	*outside*
17	*pinkie*	*little finger*
18	*provost*	*mayor*
19	*rone*	*drainpipe*
20	*rowan*	*mountain ash*
21	*to shoogle*	*to wobble, shake*
22	*to sort*	*to mend*
23	*to stay*	*to live, reside*
24	*through*	*across*
25	*wee*	*small*

Notes

1   *Ashet* is a loan word from French and is unknown in other varieties of English.

2   *Aye* is known by EngEng speakers mainly from archaic sources, songs, or nautical usage, but is never used in normal speech in the south of England. In Scotland it is informal but entirely natural.

3   *Brae* occurs frequently in place and street names, and refers to the slope of the hill, not to the entire hill.

4   EngEng speakers talk of *bramble bushes* or even *brambles* for the bushes on which blackberries grow, but ScotEng (and certain varieties in northern England) use *bramble* also for the fruit itself.

5   *Burn* is neutral in style, but is not used in England. Most EngEng speakers, however, probably know what it means. *Stream* is used in ScotEng in the figurative sense.

6   Places which sell hot food to be taken away and eaten off the premises are known in Scotland as *carry-outs*. (In the south of England they are *take-aways* and in the north *take-outs*. *Carry-out* and *take-out* are also used in North America.)

7 *Dram* is usually used with reference to whisky.

8 *Dreich* is a self-consciously Scottish word, i.e. Scots know that English people do not know it, but it is frequently heard.

9 Both *folk* and *people* are known and used in Scotland and England. *Folk*, however, is much more common and more colloquial in ScotEng: e.g. *They're very nice folk; There were a lot of folk there.* In EngEng this type of usage sounds archaic, and *folk* is used mainly as an adjective as in *folk-songs*, *folk-tale*, etc. The ScotEng usage is also found in northern England and in parts of the US. (Also, the plural *folks* can mean 'parents' or 'family, relatives' in parts of the USA.)

10 *Haar* is particularly common in the east of Scotland and refers to the thick mist that comes in from the sea.

11 Scottish hospitals are often known as *infirmaries*, but *hospital* is also common. (Infirmary is also used in the USA, usually referring to a university medical treatment unit where surgery is not performed.)

12 *Jag* (noun or verb) is frequently used in connection with thorns, injections, etc.

13 *Janitor* occurs in this usage also in NAmEng.

14 *Loch*, meaning 'lake', is familiar to most English speakers around the world, from the names of famous Scottish lakes, e.g. Loch Ness and Loch Lomond. The word is originally from Gaelic.

15 *To mind* has all the meanings in ScotEng that it has in EngEng, but it has the additional meaning, in informal usage especially, of 'to remember' as in *Do you mind when we went to Edinburgh?*

16 *Outwith* is not known in EngEng but can be frequently encountered in newspapers, public notices, etc. in Scotland.

17 *Pinkie* is not known by many EngEng speakers, but is widely used in NAmEng also.

18 The Scottish legal system is separate from that of England and Wales, and many different words are used in legal language, some of them having no counterpart in EngEng. Besides *provost* is ScotEng *procurator fiscal* which corresponds to EngEng *public prosecutor*.

19 *Rone* in ScotEng can refer to either a downward-drawing pipe outside a house or to the horizontal gutterings around the roof. EngEng speakers generally have no idea what this word means.

20 *Rowan* /rɑuən/ is known in England, but there it is normally pronounced /rouən/.

21 *To shoogle*, *shoogly* is informal but very usual in ScotEng.

22 This usage is unknown in EngEng, where *to sort* simply means 'to arrange, to classify'.

23 *Stay* has all the usual EngEng meanings in ScotEng, but it also means 'to reside, live' as in *I stay at Portobello.*

24 In discussing east-west or west-east journeys in Scotland itself, speakers often use the word *through*, as in *I'm going through to Glasgow* (from Edinburgh).

25 *Wee* is known to EngEng speakers but is not often used by them. It is extremely common in ScotEng.

One is also likely to encounter a number of phrases and idioms which are specifically Scottish. A few are listed here:

ScotEng	*EngEng*
How are you keeping?	*How are you?*
I doubt he's not coming	*I expect he's not coming*
Away to your bed	*Go to bed*
That's me away	*I'm going now*
I've got the cold	*I've got a cold*
It's for your Christmas	*It's your Christmas present*
I gave her a row	*I scolded her*
He gave me a fright	*He frightened me*
I'm finished it	*I have finished it/I'm finished*
I'll get you home	*I'll take* (accompany) *you home*
Cheerio just now!	*Cheerio* (goodbye) *for now!*
To go the messages	*To go shopping*
The back of nine o'clock	*Soon after nine o'clock*

5.2 English in Ireland

Until the seventeenth century, almost the whole of Ireland was Irish-speaking, with English speakers confined for the most part to a few towns. Native speakers of Irish are now, however, few in number and are confined to rural areas of the south-west, west and north-west, even though Irish is the official language of the Republic and is taught in schools.

The English that was originally spoken in and around Dublin was introduced for the most part from the west and west Midlands of England and still shows signs of this today. English of this sort has spread to cover most of what is today the Irish Republic.

The English of the north of Ireland, on the other hand, has its roots in Scotland, particularly the south-west of Scotland, since it was from this region that large numbers of Protestant settlers arrived, from the seventeenth century onwards. (The two main ethnic groups of Northern Ireland, today labelled 'Catholics' and 'Protestants', are thus to a large extent descendants of the original Irish-speakers and Scots-speaking settlers, respectively.) For a while, Scots-speaking areas of the far north were separated from English-speaking areas of the south by entirely Irish-speaking areas, and at the level of rural dialects there is still today a fairly sharp line that can be drawn across

Northern Ireland dividing heavily Scots-influenced Ulster-Scots varieties in the far north from other less heavily Scots-influenced Mid-Ulster varieties.

In this chapter we use the label NIrEng to refer to the ScotEng-origin varieties spoken in the north of Ireland, i.e. Ulster-Scots and Mid-Ulster English; and the label SIrEng to refer to the EngEng-origin varieties of the south of Ireland. This distinction is *not* coterminous with the political division of the Republic of Ireland and Northern Ireland: some areas of the Republic, e.g. Donegal, speak NIrEng, while some of the southern areas of Northern Ireland speak SIrEng.

5.2.1 NIrEng Pronunciation

At the level of educated speech, NIrEng pronunciation differs from that of ScotEng mainly in the following respects (many of which can be heard on the recording):

1   The vowel /e/ of *bay* may be diphthongized to [ei]. Word-finally, however, it is often [ɛ·], and pre-consonantally it may be a diphthong of the type [ɛə] ~ [iə], e.g. *gate* [giət].

2   /ɒ/ and /ɔ:/ may contrast, but only before /p, t, k/. Thus, unlike ScotEng, *cot* and *caught* are distinct, but like ScotEng, *awful* and *offal* are homophonous.

3   /ɑu/ is often rather different from its ScotEng counterpart. In NIrEng the vowel of *house* may range from [œʉ], [ɛʉ], [æʉ] to [ɐ̟ə] and even [ɜɨ]. Middle-class NIrEng can have [ɑʉ] or even [ɔʉ].

4   /r/ is usually not a flap but a frictionless continuant. Words such as *bird*, *card* are pronounced very much as in NAmEng.

5   In most NIrEng-speaking areas, /l/ is clear [l].

6   Intervocalic /t/ is not infrequently a voiced flap [ḓ], cf. NAmEng.

The intonation of certain types of NIrEng is also very distinctive and resembles that of south-western Scotland. This can be heard on the recording.

English RP exerts a certain influence on the speech of middle-class Northern Irish speakers.

5.2.2 NIrEng Grammar and Lexis

Most of the grammatical and lexical features of NIrEng which differentiate it from EngEng are also found in ScotEng and/or SIrEng (see especially 5.1.4, page 84 and 5.2.6, page 92). A distinctively NIrEng grammatical feature, however, is the use of *whenever* to refer to a single occasion, as in *Whenever my baby was born, I became depressed* ('When my baby was born ...'). North-western varieties of NIrEng also have positive *anymore* as in USEng (see 4.1.3(11), page 64).

Where NIrEng lexis differs from EngEng, it is usually the same as ScotEng or SIrEng. Of the vocabulary items cited in 5.1.5, page 86, (ScotEng), the following (at least) are also found in NIrEng: *aye, brae, burn, carry-out, folk, jag, janitor, pinkie, shoogle, wee.* The word *loch* also occurs in NIrEng but is spelt *lough.* Of the vocabulary items listed in 5.2.7, page 94, (SIrEng), *bold, cog* and *delph* can also be found in NIrEng. Other lexical items not found in EngEng include:

NIrEng	EngEng
to boke	to vomit
to gunder	to shout
to hoke	to poke around, to dig into, to rummage
to skite	to slap, to splash
to wither	to hesitate
throughother	untidy, messy

These words are also known in parts of Scotland.

In NIrEng, *bring* and *take* can be used differently than in EngEng, e.g.:

NIrEng: *You bring the children to school, and I'll take them home*
EngEng: *You take the children to school, and I'll bring them home*

(This is also true of some varieties of SIrEng and USEng. And in some parts of the west of Scotland, *take* would be used in both clauses of the above sentence, while in some USEng varieties *bring* would be used in both clauses.)

Of the Scottish idioms and phrases listed at the end of 5.1.5 (page 88), the following (at least) are also used in NIrEng: *I doubt he's not coming, I've got the cold, That's me away, I'll get you home, to go the messages.* Other NIrEng idioms include:

NIrEng	EngEng
He gets doing it	He is allowed to do it
It would take you to be there early	You have to be there early
I'm not at myself	I'm not feeling very well
You're well mended	You're looking better (after an illness)

5.2.3   SIrEng Pronunciation: Vowels

The SIrEng vowel system can be presented as follows (table 5.2) and can be heard on the recording (note that the length distinction typical of RP is also found here, while it is absent from both ScotEng and NIrEng):

Table 5.2   SIrEng Vowels

/ɪ/	[ɪ]	*bid*
/ɛ/	[ɛ]	*bed*
/æ/	[a]	*bad*
/ɒ/	[ɑ]	*pot*
/ʌ/	[ɔ˞]	*putt, nurse*
/ʊ/	[ʊ]	*put*
/iː/	[iː]	*bee, peer, very*
/ei/	[eː]	*bay, pair*
/ai/	[ɜɪ]	*buy*
/ɔi/	[ɔɪ]	*boy*
/uː/	[ʉː]	*boot, tour*
/ou/	[oː]	*boat, hoarse*
/au/	[ɜʉ]	*bout*
/ɑː/	[aː]	*path, calm, bard*
/ɔː/	[ɑː]	*paw, talk, port*
/ə/	[ə]	*sofa, wanted, horses*

The RP vowels /ɜː/, /ɪə/, /ɛə/, and /ʊə/ do not occur, since SIrEng is rhotic (cf. 5.1.1(1), page 82). Note the rounded vowel [ɔ˞] for /ʌ/.

The following points represent variable pronunciation differences:

1   Words such as *path, dance* may often have /æ/ rather than /ɑː/ (see 2.1.2(4), page 12).
2   Words such as *hoarse, mourning* may be pronounced with /ɔː/, (the same as *horse, morning*) rather than with /ou/.
3   Words such as *nurse* may be /nʊrs/ rather than /nʌrs/ = [nɔ˞ ɹs].
4   In some types of Dublin speech, words such as *pair* may be /pʌr/ = [pɔ˞ɹ] rather than /peir/.
5   Words like *book, cook, rook* may have a /uː/ rather than /ʊ/.
6   *Many, any,* etc. may be prounounced /mæniː/ rather than /mɛniː/.
7   Some words which have /ɒ/ in RP may have /ɔː/ in SIrEng (cf. NAmEng, 3.1.1(2e), page 33). These words include *dog, doll, cross, lost, often, wrong.*

At the level of uneducated speech the following pronunciations, which may also appear in the informal speech of educated speakers, can be found:

1   *tea, please, sea,* etc. with /ei/ rather than /iː/; e.g. *tea* [tʰeː]. This can also be heard in NIrEng.

2   *old, cold, bold* etc with /ɑu/ rather than /ou/; e.g. *old* [ɜʉld]. This feature is also found in NIrEng.
3   a tendency to neutralize the opposition /ai/–/ɔi/ in favour of /ai/ e.g. *oil* /ail/.

5.2.4   SIrEng Pronunciation: Consonants

1   SIrEng is rhotic. The /r/ is normally a retroflex approximant, as in NAmEng and NIrEng.
2   The contrast between /ʍ/ and /w/ is preserved: *which* /ʍič/, *witch* /wič/.
3   /l/ is clear [l] in all positions.
4   Final voiceless plosives /p, t, k/ are released, aspirated, and without glottalization. In the speech of Dublin, there may also be considerable affrication in final position: e.g. *back* [bakx], *top* [tʰapɸ].
5   The influence of Irish phonetics and phonology manifests itself in the treatment of the contrasts /t/-/θ/ and /d/-/ð/. In many varieties the contrast is not preserved, with the dentals /t̪/ and /d̪/ being used throughout. In other varieties the contrast may be preserved in ways other than that employed by RP. For example:

	tin	*thin*
RP	[tʰ]	[θ]
SIrEng	[t̪ʰ]	[t̪ʰ]
or	[tʰ]	[t̪ʰ]
or	[t̪ʰ]	[θ]
or	[θ]	[t̪θ]

(The clusters /tr/ and /dr/ are realized as [t̠r] and [d̠r] by nearly all SIrEng speakers; e.g. *drop* [d̠rapʰ]. This is true also of speakers of NIrEng.)

5.2.5   Stress in SIrEng

Distinctively SIrEng stress placement is found in a few words:

SIrEng	*EngEng*
díscipline	*díscipline*
architécture	*árchitecture*

5.2.6   SIrEng Grammar

There are a number of grammatical differences between SIrEng and EngEng. Most of the typically SIrEng forms are found only in speech, particularly in colloquial styles. They include:

1   The auxiliary *shall* is relatively rare, as in ScotEng, NIrEng and NAmEng. Instead, *will* is generally used.

2   Progressive verb forms are more frequent and are subject to fewer restrictions than in other varieties of English. For example, they can occur with many stative verbs:

> *I'm seeing it very well*
> *This is belonging to me*

3   The simple past tense is used when the sequence of tenses would require the past perfect in other English varieties:

> SIrEng: *If he saw her, he would not have done it*
> Other Eng: *If he had seen her, he would not have done it*

4   An aspectual distinction between habitual and non-habitual actions or states is signalled by placing *do*, inflected for tense and person, before the habitual verb:

Habitual	**Non-habitual (on a single occasion)**
I do be drunk	*I am drunk*
(=I am habitually drunk)	(= I am drunk now)
He does be writing	*He is writing*

5   A calque (loan-translation) from Irish involves the use of the adverb *after* with a progressive where a perfective would be used in other varieties:

> SIrEng: *I'm after seeing him*
> Other Eng: *I have just seen him*

The perfect is also avoided in other contexts:

SIrEng	**EngEng**
How long are you here?	*How long have you been here?*
Did you have your dinner yet? (cf. NAmEng, ScotEng).	*Have you had your dinner yet?*

This feature of perfect-avoidance is also typical of NIrEng.

6   *Let* can be used with second person imperatives: *let you stay here* (= 'Stay here').

7   Clefting is frequently used and is extended to use with copular verbs, which is not possible in other varieties:

> *It was very ill that he looked*
> *Is it stupid you are?*

8   Indirect questions may retain question-inversion and lack a subordinator (*if/whether*):

> SIrEng: *I wonder has he come*
> Other Eng: *I wonder if he has come*

This also occurs in NIrEng.

9   *Yes* and *no* tend to be used less frequently than in other varieties. Instead, ellipted verb phrases are used, as in Irish, e.g.:

> *Are you going?*   *I am*
> *Is it time?*   *It is*
> *Did he come?*   *He did not*

10   The conjunction *and* can be used to connect simultaneous events in all English varieties, as in *John sang and Mary played the piano*. In SIrEng it can additionally be used to connect a finite clause with a non-finite clause, and is perhaps best 'translated' into other varieties as 'when, as, while':

> SIrEng: *It only struck me and you going out of the door*
> EngEng: *It only struck me when you were going out of the door*

5.2.7   SIrEng Lexis

SIrEng vocabulary in most cases follows EngEng rather than NAmEng usage. In those respects in which it differs from EngEng, it often resembles ScotEng. In some cases lexical forms not found in other varieties are due to borrowing from Irish, while in other cases they may be due to preservation of archaic forms. Distinctively SIrEng usages include the following:

SIrEng	*EngEng*
bold	*naughty*
cog	*to cheat*
delph	*crockery*
evening	*afternoon and evening*
foostering	*fuss*
yoke	*gadget, thing*

Note also the distinctively SIrEng directional terms:

back	= westwards, in the West
below	= northwards, in the North
over	= eastwards, in the East
up above	= southwards, in the South

6
Other Varieties of English

All of the varieties of English we have discussed so far are spoken by native speakers and are the result of 'normal' historical development. In a number of parts of the world, however, we find:

(a) varieties of English or English-based speech which are the result of what is rather an unusual historical development, and
(b) varieties of English widely spoken by non-native speakers. We deal with (a) in 6.1 and (b) in 6.2 (page 99).

6.1 English-based Creoles

In certain limited contact situations between peoples who have no common language, linguistically simplified, mixed, impoverished and restricted languages known as *pidgins* may develop. Pidgins based on English have developed a number of times in a number of places, most notably in West Africa, from where they were transferred to the Caribbean, and in the Papua-New Guinea area.

Sometimes it happens that a pidgin becomes the main language of a community and acquires native speakers. If this occurs, the language is known as a *creole*, and—while it remains mixed and simplified in a technical, linguistic sense—it is no longer impoverished or restricted, as it is used by its speakers for all the purposes speakers need to use their native language for. Thus, a creole is a perfectly normal language, except that its history may be somewhat unusual. In the area of Papua-New Guinea, the creolization process (the acquisition of native speakers) is only just beginning, while in and around the Atlantic, creoles are well established. We concentrate here on the Atlantic creoles.

In some cases an English-based creole language has had no contact with English and is therefore linguistically unaffected by it (except, of course, for the original basis). If this is the case, the creole is not intelligible to English speakers. An example of this type is Sranan, the main language of Surinam (formerly Dutch Guiana). In other cases, the influence of English has been very extensive indeed, and the result is a variety of English which shows some creole influence. Examples of this type are the varieties of English spoken on St. Helena (an island in the south Atlantic), on Bermuda, and by many American Blacks.

In still other cases, we find an intermediate situation, with language varieties which in some respects resemble English and in other respects do not. This is the situation found on many of the islands of the Caribbean, the Bahamas, Guyana, Belize (formerly British Honduras), Panama, the east coasts of Honduras, Costa Rica and Nicaragua, the south Carolina and Georgia coast of the USA (where the creole is known as Gullah), and, across the Atlantic, in Sierra Leone. In some instances, particularly on the formerly British Caribbean Islands, we also find a social dialect continuum, with the upper social classes speaking English, the lower classes speaking creole, and the intermediate social strata speaking a variety in between the two.

6.1.1   West Indian English

Since the Jamaican English-Creole continuum is one of the best described, we will illustrate some of the typical characteristics of West Indian English here by reference to Jamaican English. It must be kept in mind, however, that the varieties of English and Creole spoken elsewhere in and around the Caribbean, while still being distinctively West Indian or Caribbean, do differ in a number of respects from the Jamaican variety.

Table 6.1   Jamaican Creole Vowels

/ɪ/	*pit*
/ɛ/	*pet*
/a/	*pat, pot, one, father*
/ʊ/	*put*
/o/	*putt, bird*
/iː/	*bee*
/uː/	*boot*
/aː/	*bard, law*
/oː/	*board*
/ie/	*bay, beer, bear*
/uo/	*boat, for*
/ai/	*buy, boy*
/au/	*bout*

6.1.1.1 Jamaican Creole and Jamaican English Pronunciation

A typical **Jamaican Creole** vowel system is given in table 6.1.

The following features of Jamaican Creole pronunciation can be noted:

1 There is no distinction between /a/ and /ɔ/, or beteween /ai/ and /ɔi/. Note, however, that after some initial consonants some pairs of words are still distinct as, for example:

cat	/kjat/	*boil*	/bwail/
cot	/kat/	*bile*	/bail/

2 Words ending in /aun/ in other forms of English are pronounced with /oŋ/ in Jamaican Creole, e.g. *town* /toŋ/ (the same as *tongue*).
3 Jamaican Creole is non-rhotic.
4 The Jamaican Creole consonantal system does not have the distinctions /t/-/θ/ and /d/-/ð/, with /t/ and /d/ being the only phonemes used from each pair: e.g. *thing* /tɪŋ/; *them* /dɛm/.
5 Consonant clusters are often reduced, both initially and finally, but far more extensively in final position:

scratch	/krač/
strong	/traŋ/
child	/čail/

As we go up the social scale from Creole towards **Jamaican English**, pronunciation comes to resemble more closely that of RP. In particular, the vowels of *bud* and *bird*, *pat* and *pot*, *beer* and *bear*, etc. are distinguished. Some non-RP features occur, however, even at the top of the scale. These include:

6 Jamaican English is sometimes rhotic, especially in formal styles.
7 Final consonant clusters are often reduced:

child	/čail/
tact	/tak/
wind	/wɪn/

8 Perhaps the most distinctive characteristic of Jamaican English (and indeed of many other WIEng varieties) is a difference from other varieties in stress, rhythm and intonation. Unstressed /ə/ occurs far less frequently than in EngEng:

	JamEng	*EngEng*
Jamaica	[ǰamieka]	[ǰəmeikə]
daughter	[da:ta]	[dɔ:tə]
wonderful	[wandaful]	[wʌndəfəl]

And there is a tendency for Jamaican English to be 'syllable-timed', like French, rather than 'stress-timed', like other varieties of English. This means that each syllable occurs at approximately regular intervals rather than, as in EngEng, each *stressed* syllable occurring at approximately regular intervals. This particular feature of Jamaican English renders it difficult to comprehend for those unused to the variety.

6.1.1.2   West Indian English Grammar

The grammar of West Indian creoles is very different indeed from that of Standard English. Moving up the Creole-English continuum, some creole grammatical features can still be found, especially in informal speech from the middle of the continuum. Some of these features are the following:

1   Lack of plurality marking on nouns, if the context or a quantifier makes this clear, e.g.: *five book* ('five books').

2   Lack of possessive markers on nouns: *this man brother* ('this man's brother').

3   Lack of 3rd person -*s* on verbs: *He like it* ('He likes it').

4   Lack of the copula in equational sentences and with progressives:

> *She very nice*   ('She is very nice')
> *He going home now*   ('He is going home now')

5   Lack of formally marked passives:

> *That thing use a lot*   ('That thing is used a lot')

6   Lack of tense markers on verbs; instead, tense may be marked by adverbs or periphrastically with *do* or with other particles (e.g. *bin* for past tense):

> *He walk home last night*
> *He did walk home last night* } ('He walked home last night')
> *He bin walk home last night*

7   In sentences like *He is easy to annoy*, EngEng interprets the grammatical subject (*he*) of the main verb (*easy*) as the semantic object of the subordinate verb (*annoy*); thus, the sentence can be paraphrased as *It is easy for people to annoy him*. In WI creole and WIEng the grammatical subject may also be interpreted as the semantic subject of the subordinate verb; thus, a paraphrase could be *It is easy for him to annoy people*, which has a completely different meaning.

8   In WH-word questions, subject-verb inversion may not occur:

> *What time it is?*
> *Who this is?*
> *Why you are leaving?*

6.1.1.3 West Indian Lexis

The fullest treatment of West Indian English lexis available is the *Dictionary of Jamaican English* (Cassidy & Le Page, 1980), although others are in preparation. Jamaican English words which are likely to be encountered and may cause particular difficulty include:

JamEng	*EngEng*
to carry (as in *I'll carry you home*)	*to take, transport*
dread	*terrible, excellent*
dunny	*money*
duppy	*ghost*
facety	*cheeky*
foot	*leg and foot*
ganja	*marijuana*
licks	*a beating*
to look for	*to visit*
to mash up	*to destroy, ruin, break up* (of a marriage)
peelhead	*a bald-headed person*
a something	*a thing*
to stain	*to taste sour, to be sticky*
tall	*long* (of hair)
vex	*annoyed*

People with an interest in reggae music may also encounter vocabulary and usages typical of the Rastafarian religious cult. These include:

JamEng	*EngEng*
Babylon	anything which is viewed as negative or destructive in the Western world; oppression generally
dreadlock	*tightly twisted locks of hair*
I and I	*we, you, I* (the Rastaman's pronoun of collective awareness and interest)
Jah	*God*
overstand	*understand*

6.2 Non-native Varieties of English

In many parts of the world, particularly in Africa, Malaysia, Philippines, Singapore, Hong Kong and the Indian sub-continent, English is widely used as an official language, as the language of education, and as a means of wider communication by people who are native speakers of some other language. In this section, we concentrate on English in West Africa and India, by way of illustration of non-native varieties.

While West African and Indian English do not have a significant number of native speakers, they have each acquired or are acquiring relatively consistent forms as a result of wide-spread and frequent use. However, these varieties of English differ, often considerably, from the English of native speakers elsewhere in the world, mainly as a result of interference from local languages. Thus native speakers of English may sometimes have difficulty in understanding these non-native varieties. This is something of a problem, but it is not clear what should be done about it. If, for example, certain features of West African English make that variety easier and better than EngEng for West Africans to learn and use, then does it matter that British people find WAfEng difficult to understand? After all, Americans may find ScotEng difficult to understand, but no one would seriously suggest that this is a reason for changing ScotEng. There is, however, a certain lack of parallel between the ScotEng and the WAfEng cases: (a) the Scots are native speakers, which, it can be argued, gives their variety of English a validity or legitimacy that WAfEng or IndEng may not have; and (b) many West Africans and Indians *believe* that they are speaking EngEng, or at least have the speaking of EngEng as their aim.

A particular problem arises in the case of speakers of non-native varieties of English who attempt to get English Language degrees at continental European universities. For example, a West African student's English may be more fluent than that of a Dutch student, but is the WAfEng variety valid or appropriate in the Dutch situation, and, more importantly, should such a student be allowed to teach English in a Dutch school?

There are no easy solutions to such problems. We believe, however, that as long as the deviations from EngEng in, for example, an African's or Indian's English are not great, then there is no reason to object to that variety being used in native English-speaking areas. Obviously, within Africa or India themselves, the margin for tolerance of deviation can be even wider. Equally as important, we believe that native English speakers travelling to areas such as Africa or India should make the effort to improve their comprehension of the non-native variety of English (much as Americans would have to improve their comprehension of ScotEng when travelling in Scotland) rather than argue for a more English-type English in these areas. Care should probably also be taken, however, that deviations from native English varieties should not become too great; otherwise, wider communication through English might be impaired.

6.2.1 West African English

English has a sizeable number of native speakers in South Africa, Namibia (South West Africa) and Zimbabwe, and a number in Botswana, Lesotho and Kenya. There are also some native speakers of English in Liberia, as the ruling élite there is descended from freed slaves who were returned to Africa from the USA. Elsewhere in Africa, English is widely spoken in Cameroon, Gambia, Ghana, Malawi, Nigeria, Sierra Leone, Tanzania, Uganda and Zambia.

An English-based creole, Krio, which resembles Jamaican Creole to some degree, is spoken in and around Freetown, Sierra Leone. It is spoken by descendents of (a) Blacks who were returned from London; (b) escaped slaves who fought on the British side in the American War of Independence, and who were returned to West Africa by the British (via Nova Scotia); and (c) freed Jamaican slaves. Pidgin English is widely spoken along the West African coast and in some parts of Nigeria but this, to, is creolizing. In some areas, therefore, there is a social dialect continuum ranging from pidgin or creole to West African Standard English. We shall deal here with varieties that are unambiguously English, particularly those spoken in Ghana, Nigeria and Sierra Leone.

6.2.1.1 WAfEng Pronunciation

The vowel system of WAfEng is typically reduced in comparison to that of most native varieties of English, lacking several vowel contrasts. One type of WAfEng vowel system is given in table 6.2. Different speakers show different degrees of approximation between this system and that of RP.

Table 6.2 *WAfEng Vowels*

/i/	*pit, peat*
/e/	*gate*
/ɛ/	*ten, turn*
/a/	*pat, part, father, butter*
/ɔ/	*pot, but*
/o/	*boat*
/u/	*boot, put*
/ai/	*buy*
/ɔi/	*boy*
/au/	*now*

The following features of WAfEng can be noted:

1   WAfEng is non-rhotic. Thus *ten* and *turn* are homophonous.

2   Words such as *button, apple* do not have final syllabic consonants as in other varieties of English:

	WAfEng	*RP*
button	/bɔtin/	/bʌtn̩/
apple	/apul/	/æpl̩/

3   Words ending in *mb—bomb, climb, plumb* etc.—may be pronounced with a final /b/. Similarly, words ending in *ng—ring, long, bang* etc.—may be pronounced with a final /ŋg/.
4   There is a tendency for final consonant clusters to be reduced: *last* /las/, *passed* /pas/.
5   There is a tendency for final voiced consonants to be devoiced: *proud* /praut/, *robe* /rop/.
6   A number of words have stress differences from EngEng:

> *congratuláte*
> *investigáte*
> *madám*
> *mainténance*
> *recogníze*
> *súccess*

7   Contrastive stress is rare. For example, rather than an exchange like:

> *Did John go to the store?*
> *No, Bill went*

one is more likely to find a clefted version for emphasis/focussing:

> *No, it was Bill who went*

8   WAfEng is typically syllable-timed rather than stress-timed (see 6.1.1.1 (8), page 97). This is perhaps the main cause of intelligibility difficulties for native speakers. (Intelligibility difficulties work, of course, in both directions.)

6.2.1.2   WAfEng Grammar

WAfEng varies quite considerably from place to place: some of the forms we list below, for instance, occur in Ghana but not in Nigeria, or *vice-versa*. It also varies, as does Indian English, very much according to the education of the speaker and the formality of the situation. Some of the forms given here are not, therefore, employed by the most educated speakers, or at least not in writing. Where the grammar of WAfEng differs from that of other varieties of English, this is often (but not always) due to interference from indigenous languages. This interference is most marked in less educated and more informal styles.

Typical WAfEng grammatical forms include the following:

1 Omission of articles: *I am going to cinema.*

2 Pluralization of non-count nouns:
  I lost all my furnitures
  The damages caused are great

3 The use of resumptive pronouns, not only after focussed nouns, as in some colloquial styles of English:
  My brother, he's crazy
but also in relative clauses in a non-English manner:
  The guests whom I invited them have arrived

4 No distinction between the reflexive pronoun *themselves* and the reciprocal pronoun *each other*:
  They like themselves = 'They like each other'

5 Formation of comparative clauses without using the comparative form of the adjective when it involves *more*:
  *It is the youths who are skilful in performing
    tasks than the adults*

6 Absence of infinitival *to* after some verbs: *They enabled him do it.*

7 The use of progressive aspect with *have* when expressing a temporary state: *I am having a cold.*

8 The use of a universal tag question—*is it?*—regardless of person, tense or main clause auxiliary:
  We should leave now, is it? (EngEng: *'shouldn't we?'*)
  She has gone home, is it? (EngEng: *'hasn't she?'*)

9 A non-English use of *yes* and *no* in answering questions:
  Hasn't he come home yet?
  (a) *Yes* = 'he *hasn't* come home yet'
  (b) *No* = 'he *has* come home'
cf. also: *It may not rain tomorrow*
  I hope so = 'I hope it will *not* rain'

6.2.1.3 WAfEng Lexis

Many differences in vocabulary between WAfEng and other varieties of English involve extensions or alterations to the semantic or grammatical function of English words. Others reflect usages of equivalent words from indigenous languages, while still others are innovations. The list below gives a few examples by way of illustration. Not all the items are found in all West African countries.

WAfEng	EngEng
again	*anymore*
amount	besides EngEng meaning, it can also mean *money*
balance	*change* (i.e. money returned to a customer)
a been-to	*someone who has 'been to' Europe or North America* (slightly derogatory)
to bluff	besides EngEng meaning, it can also mean *to dress fashionably* or *to show off*
carpet	*linoleum*
corner	*a bend in the road*
chop bar/canteen	*a restaurant serving indigenous food*
coal pot	*a form of brazier for cooking on*
guy	*an outgoing, self-assured young man*
to hear	besides EngEng meaning, one can also *hear*, i.e. '*understand*', a language
hot drink	*alcoholic spirits, liquor*
rice water	*rice porridge*
serviceable	besides EngEng meaning, it can also mean *willing to serve*
sorry	an expression of sympathy to someone who has just had a mishap (corresponds to similar terms in WAf languages); not very usual as an apology
the steer/steering	*the steering wheel of a vehicle*
to take in	besides EngEng meaning, it can also mean *to become pregnant*

A very distinctive characteristic of WAfEng vocabulary and grammar (and also of IndEng) is the use of 'high' literary style, i.e. the use of long or Latinate words (*epistle* instead of *letter*, *purchase* instead of *buy*) and complicated grammatical constructions not only in writing but also in speech. This could be due to several things, including exposure to literary rather than colloquial English, the prestige of the written word, and the desire *not* to sound too West African (or Indian).

6.2.2 Indian English

In the South Asian sub-continent, English is widely spoken and written in India, Pakistan, Bangladesh, and Sri Lanka. We concentrate here on India, where English is an official language and is used as one of the languages of education and wider communication. There are a number of native speakers of English in India, but these are far outnumbered by those for whom it is an additional language.

Like African English, Indian English is beset by the problem of norms (see 6.2, page 99). There is no general agreement as to whether the standard should be strictly EngEng or whether 'Indianisms' (especially in grammar) which are used by the majority of educated speakers and can also be found in newspapers should be accepted in the Indian standard.

6.2.2.1 IndEng Pronunciation

The pronunciation of Indian English varies quite considerably depending on the speaker's native language as well as on his or her educational background and degree of exposure to native English. There are, nevertheless, a number of generalizations which can be made.

1 IndEng tends to have a reduced vowel system *vis-à-vis* RP (cf. WAfEng above), with some contrasts lacking. Which contrasts these are will depend on the system of the particular native language, but often RP /ɑː/ and /ɔː/ both correspond to IndEng /ɑː/, RP /ɒ/ and /æ/ to IndEng /a/.

2 The RP diphthongs /ei/ and /ou/ tend to be monophthongal /eː/ and /oː/.

3 In southern India, word-initial front vowels tend to receive a preceding /j/ and back vowels a preceding /w/: *eight* /jeːt/: *own* /woːn/.

4 In northern India, word-initial /sk/, /st/, or /sp/ tend to receive a preceding /i/: *speak* /ispiːk/.

5 The English of most educated Indians is non-rhotic.

6 /r/ tends to be a flap [ɾ] or even a retroflex flap [ɽ].

7 In some varieties, /v/ and /w/ are not distinguished; similarly /p/ and /f/; /t/ and /θ/; /d/ and /ð/; /s/ and /š/—depending on the region.

8 The consonants /p, t, k/ tend to be unaspirated.

9 The alveolar consonants /t, d, s, l, z/ tend to be replaced by retroflex consonants /ʈ, ḍ, ṣ, ḷ, ẓ/.

10 IndEng differs considerably from other forms of English in stress, rhythm and intonation (as do WAfEng and WIEng). These differences make for difficulties, sometimes very serious indeed, in comprehension on the part of speakers of other English varieties. In particular, IndEng tends to be syllable-timed rather than stress-timed (see 6.1.1.1 (8), page 97). Also, syllables that would be unstressed in other varieties of English receive some stress in IndEng and thus do not have reduced vowels. Suffixes tend to be stressed, and function words which are weak in other varieties of English (*of* /əv/, *to* /tə/, etc.) tend not to be reduced in IndEng.

6.2.2.2   Indian English Morphology and Grammar

The following morphological and grammatical features are among
those that occur sometimes in the English of even some educated
Indians and in English-language newspapers in India:

1   Differences in count noun-mass noun distinctions:
(a) the pluralization of many EngEng mass nouns (especially
abstract nouns), e.g.:

aircrafts	'Many aircrafts have crashed there'
fruits	'We ate just fruits for lunch'
litters (rubbish)	'Do not throw litters on the street'
secrecies	'The meeting was surrounded by secrecies'
woods	'He gathered all the woods'

(b) the use of nouns alone which appear only in partitive phrases in
EngEng, e.g.:

alphabets	'He knows many alphabets already' (= letters of the alphabet)
a chalk	'Everyone pick up a chalk' (= piece of chalk)
clothes	'I have bought two clothes today' (= items of clothing)
toasts	'I'd like two toasts, please' (= pieces/slices of toast)

2   An extended use of compound formation. In EngEng,
noun + noun compounds such as *facecloth*, *teacup* can be made from
the construction noun$_1$ + *for* + noun$_2$, becoming noun$_2$ + noun$_1$ (e.g.
cup for tea becomes *teacup*). Indian English has extended this process
to include constructions with other prepositions, notably *of*. Some
compounds formed from such phrases are transparent in meaning:

chalk-piece	'piece of chalk'
God-love	'love of God'
key-bunch	'bunch of keys'
meeting notice	'notice of a meeting'

while others are ambiguous (where *of* can mean 'containing')

fish tin	'tin containing fish' (EngEng 'tin for fish')
water bottle	'bottle containing water' (EngEng 'bottle for water')

Other IndEng compounds consisting of nouns and deverbal nouns include:

age barred	'barred by age'
pindrop silence	'silent enough to hear a pin drop'
schoolgoer	'one who goes to school'

3   The use of nominal rather than participial forms of some words when used as adjectives, e.g.:

colour pencils	(EngEng: *coloured*)
schedule flight	(EngEng: *scheduled*)

4   A difference in use of prepositions in verb-preposition collocations:

(a) no preposition:

IndEng	*EngEng*
to dispense ('do without')	*to dispense with*
to strike ('delete')	*to strike out*

(b) addition of preposition:

to accompany with
to air out (one's views)
to combat against
to fear of
to return back

(c) different preposition:

IndEng	*EngEng*
to be adapted on	*to be adapted to*
to be baffled with	*to be baffled by*
to get down (from a vehicle)	*to get off/out*
to pay attention on	*to pay attention to*
to tear off/away	*to tear up*

5   The use of *itself* and *only* to emphasize time or place where EngEng speakers would usually use intonation to provide emphasis:

Can I meet with you tomorrow itself?
We will be required to have our classes here itself
Now only I have understood the problem (= just now)
We arrived today only

6   The use of adverbial *there* for 'dummy' *there*. 'Dummy' *there* in

EngEng occurs in subject position with an existential meaning and has reduced pronunciation, while adverbial *there* is not reduced: observe the difference in the two there's in *There's* (dummy) *some paper over there* (adverb). In Indian English, one can hear sentences such as the following:

> IndEng: *What do you want to eat? Meat is there, vegetables are there, bread is there*
>
> EngEng: *There is meat, there are vegetables, there is bread*
>
> IndEng: *I'm sure an explanation is there*
> EngEng: *I'm sure there is an explanation*

7   Different use of some auxiliaries. The auxiliaries *could* and *would* are often used instead of their present forms *can* and *will* because IndEng speakers feel the past forms are more tentative and thus more polite:

> *We hope that you could join us*
> *Let's finish now so that we could be there early*
> *The lecture would begin at 2:00*
> *We hope that the Vice-Chancellor would investigate this matter*

Also, *could* is used in IndEng where EngEng speakers would use *was able to*:

> *He could just only finish it before we left*
> *I could do well because I studied diligently*

The auxiliary *may* is used to express obligation politely in IndEng:

> IndEng: *This furniture may be removed tomorrow*
> EngEng: *This furniture is to be removed tomorrow*
>
> IndEng: *These mistakes may please be corrected*
> EngEng: *These mistakes should be corrected*

8   There are several differences from EngEng in the usage of tense and aspect in IndEng. They include the following:

(a) the use of the present tense with durational phrases (indicating a period from past to present) where EngEng would require the present perfect (unusual in more educated IndEng):

> IndEng: *I am here since two o'clock*
> EngEng: *I have been here since two o'clock*
>
> IndEng: *I am reading this book since (for) two hours*
> EngEng: *I have been reading this book for two hours*

(b) the use of future forms in temporal and conditional clauses where EngEng would require non-finite forms:

IndEng: *When you will arrive, please visit me*
EngEng: *When you arrive, please visit me*

IndEng: *If I will come, I will see you*
EngEng: *If I come, I will see you*

(c) a non-English use of tense sequences:

IndEng: *When I saw him last week, he told me that he is coming*
EngEng: *When I saw him last week, he told me that he was coming*

(d) the use of progressive aspect with habitual action:

IndEng: *I am doing it often*
EngEng: *I do it often*

with completed action:

IndEng: *Where are you coming from?*
EngEng: *Where have you come from?*

and with stative verbs:

IndEng: *Are you wanting anything?*
EngEng: *Do you want anything?*

IndEng: *She was having many sarees*
EngEng: *She had many sarees*

(e) the use of the perfective aspect instead of the simple past (especially with past-time adverbs):

I have been there ten years ago
We have already finished it last week
Yesterday's lecture has lasted three hours
What had you told them on Friday?
I had given it to you yesterday
We had already informed you of that

9   The absence of subject-verb inversion in direct questions, and the use of such inversion in indirect questions (which is exactly the opposite of EngEng usage):
(a) direct questions with no subject-verb inversion

IndEng: *What this is made from?*
EngEng: *What is this made from?*

IndEng: *Who you have come to see?*
EngEng: *Who have you come to see?*

IndEng: *He didn't go yesterday?*
EngEng: *Didn't he go yesterday?*

(b) indirect questions with inversion

> IndEng: *I asked him where does he work*
> EngEng: *I asked him where he works*
>
> IndEng: *I wonder where is he*
> EngEng: *I wonder where he is*

10 The use of an undifferentiated tag question—*isn't it?*—
regardless of person tense, or main clause auxiliary (see 6.2.1.2(8),
page 103):

> *You are going home soon, isn't it?*
> *They said they will be here, isn't it?*
> *We could finish this tomorrow, isn't it?*

11 Differences in complement structures with certain verbs, e.g.:

IndEng	*EngEng*
We are involved to collect poems	*We are involved in collecting poems*
She was prevented to go	*She was prevented from going*
I would like that you come	*I would like you to come*
They want that you should leave	*They want you to leave*

12 A non-English use of *yes* and *no*, as in West African English (see
6.2.1.2(9), page 103).

6.2.2.3 IndEng Lexis

One distinctive characteristic of Indian English is that there is
substantial lexical borrowing from Indian languages into English.
Some frequently encountered words include the following:

IndEng	*EngEng*
bandh	*a total strike in an area*
crore	*ten million*
dhobi	*washerman*
durzi	*tailor*
to gherao	*to demonstrate against someone by not allowing the person to leave his desk/office*
hartal	*a strike used as a political gesture* (also found in the English of Singapore and Malaysia)
lakh	*one hundred thousand*
lathi	*long heavy stick made of bamboo and bound with iron* (used by the police)

sahib	*sir, master*
swadeshi	*indigenous, native, home-grown*

Other vocabulary differences between EngEng and IndEng are due to extension or alteration of meaning of EngEng words, retention of archaic forms, or innovations. A brief sample follows:

IndEng	*EngEng*
almirah	*a chest of drawers* (from Portuguese)
appreciable	*appreciated*
as such	*consequently, therefore*
backside	*behind, in back of*
biodata	*curriculum vitae*
co-brother	*wife's sister's husband*
colony	*residential area; apartment building*
cousin-sister	*female cousin*
to demit	*to resign*
eve-teasing	*teasing girls*
to extern	*to exile, banish*
furlong	$\frac{1}{8}$ *of a mile* (archaic in EngEng except in horse-racing)
to half-fry	*to fry* (an egg) *on one side*
hotel	*restaurant, cafe* (not necessarily with lodgings)
jawan	*soldier*
to be out of station	*to be away from place of work*
playback artiste	*professional singer who sings offstage while performer on stage mimes the words*
police firing	*shooting by police*
ryot	*farmer*
stepney	*a spare wheel; a substitute*
stir	*a demonstration; agitation*
tiffin	*lunch*

Glossary

affricate consonant characterized by the gradual release of air after a complete closure.

allophone a particular realization (pronunciation) of a *phoneme* (vid.).

alveolar consonant produced by the tip or blade of the tongue touching the alveolar ridge (the ridge behind the upper teeth).

anaphoric referring back to some previous word(s) or meaning.

apical manner of articulation of a consonant using the tip of the tongue.

approximant consonant produced by two articulatory organs approaching each other without causing audible friction.

aspect the marking on the verb or auxiliary indicating duration or completion of activity: e.g. progressive aspect (-*ing*) and perfective aspect (*have* + tense + participal).

aspirated manner of articulation of a consonant whereby an audible rush of air accompanies the production of the consonant.

causative a verb or clause expressing causation.

clefting the grammatical process of focusing on an item by moving it to the front of its clause and preceding it by *it is/was/etc.*: e.g. *John bought a bicycle* can be clefted as *It was John who bought a bicycle* or *It was a bicycle that John bought*.

collocation refers to words that habitually co-occur.

complement in general, all elements of the predicate other than the verb.

continuant a consonant produced by incomplete closure of the vocal tract.

copula a stative verb which links or equates the subject and *complement* (vid.), e.g. *be*.

co-referential refers to two words that have the same reference.

count noun a noun whose referent is seen as a discrete, countable entity (opposite of *mass noun*, vid.); it can occur with an article and has a plural form.

creole a *pidgin* language (vid.) which has acquired native speakers.

dark l an *l* produced with *velarized* articulation (vid.).

deverbal noun   a noun derived from a verb.

diacritic   a mark added to a letter or symbol indicating a change in its usual pronunciation.

ellipsis   the omission of part of a sentence's structure which is recoverable from context.

epistemic   refers to a *modal* (vid.) which asserts that a proposition is known or believed to be true.

existential   refers to the use of *there* (*is*) to express existence (as opposed to location).

flap   manner of articulation (here of *d* and *r*) whereby the tip of the tongue makes a single rapid contact with the *alveolar* ridge.

fricative   consonant produced by two articulatory organs coming close enough together to cause audible friction.

glottalized   manner of articulation whereby the glottis (opening between the vocal cords) is constricted.

homophones   words with the same pronunciation but different meaning.

intervocalic   occurring between two vowels.

lateral   manner of articulation whereby air escapes around the sides of a closure, as in /l/.

mass noun   a noun whose referent is seen as being non-discrete, having no natural bounds (e.g. *air*, *happiness*); it cannot occur with an article and does not have a plural form.

modal   refers to auxiliaries used to express speaker attitudes to the proposition (e.g. obligation, certainty, possibility).

morpheme   minimal unit of meaning, used in the composition of words.

neutralization   the loss of distinction between two *phonemes* in a particular linguistic environment.

palatalized   manner of articulation whereby the blade of the tongue approaches or touches the hard palate.

partitive phrase   a phrase usually of the form $noun_1 + of + noun_2$ with the approximate meaning 'UNIT of ENTITY': e.g. *loaf of bread*.

periphrastic   using separate words rather than inflections to express some grammatical relationship.

phoneme   minimal distinctive unit of sound (the substitution in a word of one phoneme for another causes a change in meaning).

pidgin   a linguistically simplified, mixed and restricted language used in limited contact situations between people who have no common language.

plosive   consonant characterized by complete closure of the vocal tract followed by the sudden release of air.

quantifier   a word expressing quantity.

resumptive pronoun   a pronoun which marks the place of a noun that has been moved elsewhere in the sentence.

retroflex manner of articulation whereby the tip of the tongue is curled back behind the alveolar ridge.

semi-auxiliary words which have some properties of auxiliaries and some of verbs.

stative verb a verb which denotes a state of being, relational process or perceptual process rather than an action.

subordinator a conjunction which introduces a subordinate, or dependent, clause.

syllabic consonant a consonant that can occur alone to form a syllable, as /n/ in *button*.

tag question a question consisting of an auxiliary and pronoun attached to the end of a statement.

velarized manner of articulation whereby the back of the tongue contacts the velum (soft palate).

voicing refers to the vibration of the vocal cords: *voiced* sounds are produced with the vocal cords vibrating, while *voiceless* sounds are produced without them vibrating.

For further explication of these and other linguistic terms, the reader is referred to David Crystal's *A First Dictionary of Linguistics and Phonetics*, London: André Deutsch, 1980.

Selected References and Further Reading

General

BÄHR, D. 1974: *Standard Englisch und seine geographischen Varianten*. Munich: Wilhelm Fink. (A general work on varieties of English)
WELLS, J. C. 1982: *Accents of English*. Cambridge: CUP. (An excellent and exhaustive three-volume work on the pronunciation of English around the world.)

History of English—Recent Developments

BAUGH, A. C. 1957: *A History of the English Language*. 2nd edition. New York: Meridith. (Chapters 10–11.)
FOSTER, B. 1968: *The Changing English Language*. London: Macmillan.
PYLES, T. 1971: *The Origins and Development of the English Language*. 2nd edition. New York: Harcourt Brace Jovanovich. (Chapters 9–11; especially for Eng-US differences, including intonation, and vocabulary.)
STRANG, B. M. H. 1970: *A History of English*. London: Methuen. (Part I, section 2, and Part II, section 1.)

EngEng

FOWLER, H. W. 1965: *A Dictionary of Modern English Usage*. 2nd edition. Oxford: OUP.
FOWLER, W. S. 1972: *Dictionary of Idioms*. London: Nelson.
GIMSON, A. C. 1980: *An Introduction to the Pronunciation of English*. 3rd edition. London: Edward Arnold. (Description of the RP accent.)
HUGHES, A. and TRUDGILL, P. 1979: *English Accents and*

Dialects: An Introduction to Social and Regional Varieties of British English. London: Edward Arnold. (Variation in standard and non-standard types in the UK, with tape recording)
PHYTHCAN, B. A. 1979: *A Concise Dictionary of English Idioms*. London: Hodder and Stoughton.
QUIRK, R., GREENBAUM, S., LEECH, G. and SVARTVIK, J. 1972: *A Contemporary Grammar of English*. Harmondsworth: Longman. (A detailed description of Standard British English.)
SEIDL, G. 1978: *English Idioms and How to Use Them*. 4th edition. Oxford: OUP.
WOOD, F. T. 1967: *English Prepositional Idioms*. London: Macmillan.
WOOD, F. T. and HILL, R. 1979: *Dictionary of English Colloquial Idioms*. London: Macmillan.

AusNZEng

BAKER, S. J. 1966: *The Australian Language*. 2nd edition. Sydney: Curranan.
BURGESS, O. 1973: Intonation Patterns in Australian English. *Language and Speech* 16, pp. 314–26.
MITCHELL, A. G., and DELBRIDGE, A. 1965: *The Pronunciation of English in Australia*. Sydney: Angus and Robertson.
RAMSON, W. 1970: *English Transported*. Canberra: A. N. U. Press (English in Australia and New Zealand.)
TURNER, G. 1966: *The English Language in Australia and New Zealand*. Harmondsworth: Longman.

SAfEng

LANHAM, L. 1967: *The Pronunciation of South African English*. Cape Town: Balkema.
LANHAM, L. and MACDONALD, C. 1979: *The Standard in South African English and its Social History*. Heidelberg: Groos.

WEng

CONNOLLY, J. H. 1982: On the segmental phonology of a South Welsh accent of English. *Journal of the International Phonetic Association* 11, pp. 51–61.
THOMAS, A. R. 1982: Welsh English. In Trudgill, P. (ed.), *Language in the British Isles*. Cambridge: CUP.

USEng

ALLEN, H. and UNDERWOOD, G. 1971: *Readings in American Dialectology*. New York: Appleton-Century-Crofts. (Variation in American English.)

DILLARD, J. 1972: *Black English*. New York: Random House. (American Black Vernacular English.)

FRANCIS, N. 1958: *The Structure of American English*. New York: Ronald Press.

HORWILL, H. 1944: *A Dictionary of Modern American Usage*. 2nd edition. Oxford: OUP.

NICHOLSON, M. 1957: *A Dictionary of American English Usage*. New York: OUP. (Based on H. W. Fowler's *A Dictionary of Modern English Usage*.)

SHUY, R. W. 1967: *Discovering American Dialects*. Champaign, Illinois: NCTE.

STREVENS, P. 1972: *British and American English*. London: Collier-Macmillan.

ŠVEJCER, A. 1978: *Standard English in the United States and England*. The Hague: Mouton. (Includes a short section on Eng-US intonation differences.)

WILLIAMSON, J. and BURKE, V. 1971: *A Various Language*. New York: Holt, Rinehart and Winston. (Variation in American English.)

CanEng

AVIS, W. S., CRATE, C., DRYSDALE, P., LEECHMAN, D., SCARGILL, M. H. and LOVELL, C. O., 1967: *A Dictionary of Canadianisms on Historical Principles*. Toronto: W. J. Gage.

CHAMBERS, J. K. 1975: *Canadian English: Origins and Structures*. London: Methuen.

CHAMBERS, J. K. 1979: Canadian English. In Chambers, J. K. (ed.), *The Languages of Canada*. Paris: Didier.

ORKIN, M. M. 1970: *Speaking Canadian English*. Toronto: General.

ScotEng and IrEng

AITKEN, A. and McARTHUR, T. 1979: *Languages of Scotland*. Edinburgh: Chambers.

AITKEN, A. 1982: Scots Dialects and Accents. In Trudgill, P. (ed.): *Language in the British Isles*. Cambridge: CUP.

BLISS, A. 1982: Irish English. In Trudgill, P. (ed.): *Language in the British Isles*. Cambridge: CUP.

HARRIS, J. 1982: English in the north of Ireland. In Trudgill, P. (ed.), *Language in the British Isles*. Cambridge: CUP.
O'MUIRITHE, D. (ed.) 1977: *The English Language in Ireland*. Cork: Mercier.

English Pidgins and Creoles

BAILEY, B. 1966: *Jamaican Creole Syntax*. Cambridge: CUP.
CASSIDY, F. and LE PAGE, R. 1980: *Dictionary of Jamaican English*. Cambridge: CUP.
LE PAGE, R. and DE CAMP, D. 1960: *Jamaican Creole*. London: Macmillan.
REINECKE, J., TSUZAKI, S., DE CAMP, D., HANCOCK, J., WOOD, R. 1975: *Bibliography of Pidgin and Creole Languages*. Honolulu: University Press of Hawaii.

Non-Native Varieties of English

ANGOGO, R. and HANCOCK, I. 1980: English in Africa: Emerging standards or diverging regionalisms?. *English World Wide* 1, pp. 67–96.
KACHRU, B. 1969: English in South Asia. In Sebeok, T. (ed.), *Current Trends in Linguistics V*. The Hague: Mouton.
KACHRU, B. 1982: *Other Tongue: English in Non-Native Contexts*. Cambridge: CUP.
NIHALANI, P., TONGUE, R. K. and HOSALI, P. 1979: *Indian and British English: A Handbook of Usage and Pronunciation*. Oxford: OUP.
PLATT, J. and WEBER, H. 1980: *English in Singapore and Malaysia*. Oxford: OUP.
SPENCER, J. 1971: *The English Language in West Africa*. London: Longman.

The Recording

1 RP: Table 2.1, page 10
RP: The Reading Passage

2 Australian English: Table 2.3, page 17
Australian English: The Reading Passage

3 New Zealand English: Table 2.3, page 17
New Zealand English: The Reading passage

4 South African English: Table 2.4, page 25
South African English: The Reading Passage

5 Welsh English: Table 2.5, page 28
Welsh English: The Reading Passage

6a US English (Eastern): Table 3.1, page 31
US English (Eastern): The Reading Passage

6b US English (Mid-Western): Table 3.1, page 31
US English (Mid-Western): The Reading Passage

7 Canadian English: Table 3.1, page 31
Canadian English: The Reading Passage

8 Scottish English: Table 5.1, page 82
Scottish English: The Reading Passage

9 Northern Irish English: Table 5.1, page 82
Northern Irish English: The Reading Passage

10 Southern Irish English: Table 5.2, page 91
Southern Irish English: The Reading Passage

11 West Indian English: Table 2.1, page 10
West Indian English: The Reading Passage

12 West African English: Table 2.1, page 10
West African English: The Reading Passage

13 Indian English: Table 2.1, page 10
Indian English: The Reading Passage

Notes

The RP speaker demonstrates the features more typical of younger RP speakers. See especially points 1 and 4 on pages 10 and 11.

The West Indian speaker is from the island of Dominica.

The West African speaker is from Ghana and is a native speaker of Twi.

The Indian speaker is a native speaker of Tamil, a southern Indian language.

The same reading passage is used for all the varieties in the recording in order to facilitate comparison. Some speakers have made minor changes in the text to conform to the norms of their particular variety. All speakers on the tape are university or college educated.

The Reading Passage

(from Trudgill, P. 1975: *Accent, Dialect and the School* pages 15–16. London: Edward Arnold.)

As a language changes, it may well change in different ways in different places. No one who speaks a particular language can remain in close contact with *all* the other speakers of that language. Social and geographical barriers to communication as well as sheer distance mean that a change that starts among speakers in one particular locality will probably spread only to other areas with which these speakers are in close contact. This is what has happened over the centuries in the case of the languages we now call English and German. Two thousand years ago the Germanic peoples living in what is now, for the most part, Germany could understand one another perfectly well. However, when many of them migrated to England they did not remain in close contact with those who stayed behind. The result, to simplify somewhat, was that different linguistic changes took place in the two areas independently so that today English and German, while clearly related languages, are not mutually intelligible. There was presumably a certain amount of inevitability about this process, since speakers usually need to remain intelligible only to those people they normally communicate with, and, until quite recently, close and frequent communication between England and Germany was not possible. But this also means that the same kind of process is unlikely to be repeated in such an extreme form in the case of different variants of modern English. American and British English have been geographically separated, and diverging linguistically, for 300 years or so, but the divergence is not very great because of the density of the communication between the two speech communities, particularly since the advent of modern transport and communication facilities. In other words, linguistic change in English will continue, but it is very unlikely indeed (barring prolonged world-wide catastrophes) that this will lead to a decrease in the mutual intelligibility of different varieties of English. That is, it is not legitimate to argue that change in English is a bad thing because it will lead to a breakdown in communication. It will not—so long as all English speakers need and are able to keep in touch with each other.

In fact, if anything, the reverse is more likely, since change does not necessarily take place in a 'divergent' direction. Where two groups of speakers develop closer social contacts than they previously had, their language is quite likely to converge. This appears to have happened in Jamaica, where the language spoken today is much more like British English than it was 200 years ago.

And even where change is of the divergent type, it should not necessarily be assumed that this is a bad thing. From many points of view, of course, it is true that a large increase in linguistic diversity on a world-wide scale would be unfortunate. Particularly in the sphere of international politics, it is desirable that different peoples should be able to communicate as freely and accurately as possible. But at the same time it is also valid to argue that the maintenance of a certain number of linguistic barriers to communication is a good thing. These barriers, although penetrable, ensure the survival of different language communities. And the separation of the world's population into different groups speaking different languages helps the growth of cultural diversity, which in turn can lead to opportunities for the development of alternative modes of exploring possibilities for social, political and technological progress. A world where everyone spoke the same language could be a very dull and stagnant place.

Index

/i/ 31, 32, 37, 40, 82–3, 101, 105
/i:/ 10–12, 16, 17, 24, 25, 28, 36, 40,
   91, 96
/ie/ 96
/ɪ/ 10–12, 16–19, 24, 25, 28, 31, 32,
   36–40, 82–3, 91, 96
/ɪə/ 10, 15, 17, 19, 25, 28, 34–5, 82,
   91

/ɛ/ 10, 11, 17, 19, 25, 28, 31, 36–8,
   82–3, 91, 96, 101
/ɛi/ 27, 28
/ɛə/ 10, 11, 15, 17, 19, 25, 28, 34, 82,
   91
/ɜ:/ 10, 15, 17, 25, 28, 34, 82, 91

/a/ 38, 82, 96, 101, 105
/a:/ 96
/æ/ 10, 12, 16–19, 25, 27, 28, 31–4,
   36–40, 82, 91, 105
/ai/ 10, 11, 17–19, 25, 28, 31, 32, 37,
   39–41, 82, 83, 91–2, 96, 101
/aiə/ 10
/au/ 83, 96, 101
/ɑ/ 27, 31–3, 37, 39
/ɑ:/ 10, 12, 15–18, 24, 25, 27, 28,
   32–4, 38, 40, 82, 91, 105
/ɑu/ 10, 11, 17, 25, 28, 31, 32, 35, 37,
   39, 82, 89, 91, 92
/ɑuə/ 10, 17
/ɒ/ 10, 11, 17–19, 25, 27, 28, 31–4,
   38, 40, 83, 89, 91, 105

/ɔ/ 31–3, 35–7, 82, 83, 96, 101
/ɔ:/ 10, 11, 15, 17, 18, 25, 28, 33, 35,
   83, 89, 91, 105

/ɔə/ 10, 11
/ɔi/ 10, 17, 25, 28, 31, 37, 82–3, 91–2,
   96, 101
/ɔu/ 11, 28

/u/ 31, 32, 82–3, 101
/u:/ 10–12, 17, 19, 25, 28, 37, 82, 91,
   96
[ʉ:] 11, 12
/uo/ 96
/ʊ/ 10, 17, 25, 28, 29, 31, 37, 82, 91,
   96
/ʊə/ 10, 11, 28, 34, 82, 91

/ʌ/ 10, 17, 25, 27, 28, 31, 36–7, 40,
   82–3, 91

/e/ 82, 89, 101
/e:/ 105
/ei/ 10, 17, 25, 28, 31, 32, 35–7,
   39–40, 89, 91, 105
/ɛi/ 18
/ə/ 10–12, 15, 16, 19, 24, 27, 31, 32,
   36–7, 39, 91, 96

/o/ 11, 27, 82, 96, 101
/o:/ 96, 105
/ou/ 10–12, 17, 19, 25, 28, 31, 33, 35,
   37, 39, 91–2, 105
/oʊ/ 35

[θu] 11
[ɸʉ] 11

/č/ 13, 25
[č] 18, 26

/d/ 35, 92, 96, 105
/ð/ 92, 96, 105
/d̦/ 92
/dj/ 18, 26, 38
/f/ 11, 12, 33, 34, 105
/g/ 29, 33
/h/ 13
/j/ 11, 38, 105
[j] 18, 26
/k/ 19, 25, 83, 89, 92, 105
/kw/ 19
/l/ 11–13, 19, 25, 29, 35, 83, 89, 92, 105
/ɬ/ 29
[ɬ] 13
/m/ 13
/mp/ 12
/n/ 35
/nd/ 12
/ns/ 12

/nš/ 12
/nt/ 12
/p/ 25, 83, 89, 92, 105
/r/ 13–15, 18, 19, 25–6, 28, 32–4, 36, 38–9, 82–3, 89, 92, 105
/s/ 11, 12, 33, 34, 105
/š/ 24, 41, 105
/t/ 11, 13, 18, 25, 35, 83, 89, 92, 96, 105
/ț/ 92
/θ/ 11, 12, 33, 34, 92, 96, 105
/tj/ 18, 26, 38
/v/ 105
/w/ 13, 83, 92, 105
/ʌʌ/ 13, 19, 83, 92
/x/ 29, 83
/z/ 105
/ž/ 18, 41
[ʔ] 13, 35, 83

aboriginal languages, 20
accent, 1; Received Pronunciation, 2, 9–15
accommodation, 59
adjectives, 63, 65, 107
'advanced' RP, 10, 12
adverbs, 63–5, 68
Africa, 3; English as an official language, 99; second-language varieties of English, 7; *see also* South African English
African loan-words, 74
Afrikaans, 24, 25, 26–7
all, 61
all the, 63
American Black Vernacular English, 5–7, 39, 96
American Indian loan-words, 74
anymore, 64–5
archaisms, 74, 94, 111
articles, 60–1
as well, 65
Asia, 3
Atlantic pidgins and creoles, 5, 95–6
attributes, order of, 61–2

Australian English (AusEng), 3, 4, 15–23
auxiliary verbs, 46–52, 84, 108

Bahamas, 96
Bangladesh, 104
Bantu, 24
BBC, 2, 15
Belize, 96
Bermudian English, 5, 96
Boston, 35, 38
Botswana, 101
bring and *take*, 90
'British English', 1
British Honduras, 96
'broad' accents, 16, 17
Buffalo, 39
Burns, Robert, 81, 85

Cameroon, 101
Canadian English (CanEng), 2, 4, 15, 36–8, 42, 64, 65, 74
'Canadian raising', 39
Caribbean English, 96
Caribbean pidgins and creoles, 5, 95, 96

Cassidy, F., 99
Central America, 5
Central East Coast American
    English, 31–6, 37
Chicago, 39
Cleveland, 39
collective nouns, 20, 58–9
colloquial vocabulary, Australian,
    20–1, 23; New Zealand, 23–4
come and *go*, 54–5
'conservative' RP, 10, 11, 12
consonants, Australian English, 18;
    Indian English, 105; North
    American English, 35–6;
    Received Pronunciation, 12–15;
    Scottish English, 83; South
    African English, 25–6; Southern
    Ireland English, 92; Welsh
    English, 28–9; West African
    English, 102
Costa Rica, 96
could and *would*, 108
count nouns, 59, 106
creoles and pidgins, 5–7, 95–9, 101

dare and *need*, 48–9
decide, 56
derivational verbs, 45–6
Detroit, 39
dialect, 1
different, 63
do, 20, 26, 49, 93
do-substitution, 51–2
Dominican Republic, 5–7
Donegal, 89
Dublin, 88
Dutch Guiana, 96

East New England USEng, 15
English English (EngEng), defined,
    2–3; grammatical differences
    from North American English,
    43–68; pronunciation differences
    from North American English,
    32–6, 40–2; Received
    Pronunciation, 2, 9–15; second
    language varieties, 7; spread of,
    4–7

ever, 65

Falkland Islands, 5
formal styles, 1
Freetown, Sierra Leone, 101
French loan-words, 41
future tense, 108–9

Gaelic, 81
Gambia, 101
Georgia, 38, 96
Ghana, 101, 102
Gimson, A. C., 9, 10
glottal reinforcement, 13, 35
glottal stop, 13
gotten, 45
grammar, Australian and New
    Zealand English, 19–20; Indian
    English, 106–9; North American
    English, 4, 43–68; Northern
    Ireland English, 89–90; Scottish
    English, 84–5; South African
    English, 26; Southern Ireland
    English, 92–4; Standard English,
    1; Welsh English, 29–30; West
    African English, 102–3; West
    Indian creole, 98; West Indian
    English, 98
Gullah, 96
Guyana, 96

half, 61
have, 20, 84, 103
have, *do have* and *have got*, 49–50
'high' literary style, 104
Honduras, 96
Hong Kong, 99
Hughes, A., 9, 27
hypothetical clauses, 57

idioms, Scottish English, 88
if, 57
Illinois, 37, 38
in future, 61
Indian English, 7, 99–100, 102,
    104–11
Indian languages, 110–11
inflectional verbs, 43–5
informal styles, 1

inning, 60
intonation, Indian English, 105;
    Northern Ireland English, 89
intrusive /r/, 14–15
Irish English, 4, 15, 52, 88–94
Irish language, 88, 93
irregular verbs, 44–5
is it?, 26
isn't it?, 29
itself, 107

Jamaican Creole, 96–7, 101
Jamaican English, 7, 96–8, 99
jargon, 45
journalistic English, 60, 61–2

Kenya, 24, 101
Krio, 101

Latin America, 2, 5
Latinate words, 104
Le Page, R., 99
Lesotho, 101
let's, 56
lettuce, 59
Liberia, 5, 101
like, 54
linking /r/, 14, 15
literary style, 104
loan-words, African, 74; American
    Indian, 74; French, 41;
    Portuguese, 111; Spanish, 74;
    USEng, 74; Yiddish, 74
London, 17

McDiarmid, Hugh, 85
Malawi, 101
Malaysia, 7, 99, 110
mass nouns, 59, 106
may, 108
mayn't, 49
Mid-Western America, 15, 36, 65
'mild' accents, 16, 17
momentarily, 64
must, 47–8

Namibia, 24, 101
need, 84–5
New Hebrides, 5

New England, 36, 38
New York City, 15, 35, 36, 38, 39,
    64–5
New Zealand English (NZEng), 3,
    4, 15–16, 18–20, 23–4
next day, 61
Nicaragua, 96
Nigeria, 101, 102
no (non-negative), 26
non-prevocalic /r/ 15
non-rhotic accents, 13–14
North America, pidgins and creoles,
    5
North American English
    (NAmEng), 2–3, 4, 31–42, 43–79
North Carolina, 38
North-west English English, 47–8
Northern Ireland English (NIrEng),
    4, 88–90
not, 84
noun class, 58–60
noun phrases, 57–8
nouns, collective, 20, 58–9; Indian
    English, 106–7

Ohio, 38
one and *you*, 62
only, 107
Ontario, 65
ordinals, 64
Otago, 19
ought to, 48

Pacific pidgins and creoles, 5
Pakistan, 104
Panama, 96
Papua New Guinea, 5, 95
past participle, 44–5
past tense, 44–5, 57, 93
Pennsylvania, 64–5
perfect tense, 93
periphrastic phrases, 56
Philippines, 99
pidgin English, 5, 101
pidgins and creoles, 5–7, 95–9, 101
plural nouns, 58–60
Portuguese loan-words, 111
possessive pronouns, 62–3
prepositions, 65–8, 107

present perfect, 57, 108
present tense, 44–5, 108
presently, 64
pronouns, 62–3
pronunciation, 1; Australian
    English, 18; Indian English, 105;
    Jamaican Creole, 97; Jamaican
    English, 97–9; New Zealand
    English, 18–19; North American
    English, 31–42; Northern Ireland
    English, 89; Received
    Pronunciation, 2, 9–15; Scottish
    English, 81–4; Southern Ireland
    English, 90–2; varieties of
    English, 4–5; West African
    English, 101–2
Public Schools, 2
punctuation, 73

quantitative nouns, 60

'r-ful' accents, 13–14
'r-less' accents, 13–14
Rastafarian cult, 99
real, 63
Received Pronunciation (RP), 2,
    9–15, 16
reciprocal pronouns, 62
regional variations, Australian and
    New Zealand English, 16; North
    American English, 31, 36–9, 43
Rhode Island, 38
rhotic accents, 13–14
rhythm, Indian English, 105
river, 62
Rochester, 39

St. Helena, 5, 96
Scots language, 4
    81, 85, 88–9
Scottish English (ScotEng), 4, 15,
    52, 81–8, 90, 100
Scottish Highlands, 27, 81
'sensational' spellings, 72
shall, 19, 46, 93
she, 20
shrimp, 60
Sierra Leone, 96, 101
Singapore, 99, 110

slang, Australian, 23
'smoothing', 11
social class, 2, 9, 96
Solomon Islands, 5
South African English (SAfEng), 3,
    4, 15–16, 24–7, 101
South Australia, 16
South Carolina, 38, 96
South-east America, 15, 36, 37
South EngEng, 15
South West Africa, 24, 101
Southern Ireland English (SIrEng),
    89, 90–4
Southern America, 38
Southland, New Zealand, 19
Spanish loan-words, 74
spelling, differences between
    EngEng and USEng, 69–72
sport, 59
Sranan, 95–6
Sri Lanka, 104
Standard English, defined, 1;
    varieties, 1–3
stress, Indian English, 105; North
    American English, 41–2;
    Southern Ireland English, 92;
    West African English, 102
'stress-timed' languages, 98
strong verbs, 44–5
subjunctive, 56–7
subordinators, 68
Surinam, 96
'syllable-timed' languages, 97–8,
    102, 105

Tanzania, 101
Texas, 36
that-clauses, 56–7
there, 107–8
to be, 55, 64
too, 29
Tristan da Cunha, 5
Trudgill, P., 9, 27

Uganda, 101
Ulster-Scots, 88–9
United States, creoles, 96
United States English (USEng), 2,
    4, 31–42, 45–50, 53–79

used to, 19–20, 48

velarization, 13
verb phrase substitutions, 51–2
verb phrases, 53–7
verbs, English English, 43–52;
    Indian English, 108–9; North
    American English, 43–52;
    Scottish English, 84–5
Virginia, 38
vocabulary, Australian English,
    20–3; Indian English, 110–11;
    New Zealand English, 23–4;
    NAmEng, 43, 73–9; Northern
    Ireland English, 90; Scottish
    English, 85–8; South African
    English, 26–7; Southern Ireland
    English, 94; Standard English, 1;
    Welsh English, 30; West African
    English, 103–4; West Indian
    English, 99
vowels, Australian English, 16–18;
    Indian English, 105; Jamaican
    Creole, 97; near-RP accents,
    11–12; North American English,
    31–5; Received Pronunciation,
    10–11; Scottish English, 81–3;
    South African English, 24–5;

Southern Ireland English, 90–2;
    Welsh English, 27–8; West
    African English, 101

want and *need*, 55, 85
Webster, Noah, 69
Wells, J. C., 10, 11, 27
Welsh English (WEng), 4, 27–30
Welsh language, 4, 30
West Africa, pidgins, 95
West African English (WAfEng), 5,
    7, 100–4
West Indian Creole, 98
West Indian English (WIEng), 96–9
whenever, 89
will, 29, 84, 93
with, 19
wonder, 56
would, 46–7

yes and *no*, 94, 103, 110
yet and *still*, 64, 85
Yiddish loan-words, 74

Zambia, 24, 101
zero plurals, 59–60
Zimbabwe, 24, 101
Zulu, 26